Contemporary Chic

Rozemarijn de Witte
Photography by Hotze Eisma

conran
OCTOPUS

Contemporary Chic

First published in Great Britain in 1997 by
Conran Octopus Limited, 37 Shelton Street,
London WC2H 9HN
Reprinted 1998

Commissioning editor Denny Hemming
Project editor Helen Ridge
Copy editor Alison Bolus
Editorial assistant Tanya Robinson
Consultant for chapter 5 Michael Holmes
Typesetting Olivia Norton
Illustrator Edith Buenen
Production Julian Deeming
Translated from the Dutch by Stephen Challacombe for
First Edition Translations Ltd, Cambridge
Index compiled by Indexing Specialists, Hove, East Sussex
A catalogue record for this book is available from the
British Library

ISBN 1 85029 925 0

Colour reproduction by Koninklijke Smeets Offset
in Weert
Printed in China

Contents

Contemporary Chic

CHAPTER 1

Natural

Creating a natural home

The natural look for the home is created by using colours drawn from nature, such as **sand, rich earth shades, white and a hint of yellow.** Of course, natural materials also belong in this decorative scheme: linen, fresh cotton, cane, wicker and wood. The great thing about using natural colours is that they allow plenty of freedom of choice in the **look and design** of your furniture, so that whether you choose country, modern or colonial-style pieces, the end result will always be **restful and warm.**

Natural

From simple to country style

1

CONTENTS

Natural

Right
THE NATURAL COLOUR PALETTE

These colours are derived from natural objects in their purest form. The possibilities within this range are vast and the paint colours shown here represent a mere sample of those available. After all, which colours do *you* find natural? Is it creamy unbleached linen or golden barley rustling in the breeze? Is it unvarnished pine, rainwashed grey pebbles or a fox's tawny coat? Most important is combining your colours successfully.

Natural

For a sense of comfort

Wood is an indispensable element in the natural interior, adding warmth where little other colour is used. **Creamy fabrics such as linen blend well with wood, especially for an informal look.** The type of furniture is less important since a relaxed yet sophisticated style, as shown here, or a more country look, achieved with wooden or wicker furniture, can be equally effective. **The natural look gives plenty of scope for the personal touch.**

SPACIOUS LIVING

The natural home should have a sense of spaciousness. This is possible in a small home by using fewer but larger pieces of furniture – an immense gilded mirror, for example, to create an illusion of space, a large and inviting sofa, and curtains sweeping down to the floor.

MAKING YOUR OWN CURTAINS

These simple linen curtains complement the varnished deal floor and the bleached colours of the furniture. They are made by sewing two layers of fabric together: an outer layer of linen and a lining of unbleached cotton. The result is heavy curtains that create a feeling of luxury.

The natural styles

Left
PAINTED CHIC

These pages show how varied the natural look can be: the country style on the one hand, compared with a restrained, modern look on the other. Here, the wooden fireplace surround has been given a coat of gloss paint. The chimney in this type of 1930s house was usually designed for gas fires, and so a large open hearth will normally not draw well. To create a draught, a ventilator has been fitted to the top of the chimney and a glass plate positioned in the fireplace.

Right
A DIVIDING WALL OF WOOD

A plain wall of Douglas fir veneer separates the dining area from the kitchen and hallway. The table is of the same colour wood, thus creating visual harmony. The natural sobriety is echoed in the row of bottles, each with a single, deep pink tulip.

SHUTTERS AS SCREENS
Wooden window shutters can be used as screens or, as here, to add interest to a wall. They contribute to the feeling of spacious living, and the out-sized church candles are ideally suited to this theme. The marble fireplace, originally black, has been decorated with matt paint, to which sand has been added, to give the appearance of sandstone.

An eye-catching table

A room decorated to echo the mood of a manor house, or an empty space except for a table and some chairs: these are the two extremes, **classical and modern.** Yet the natural look blends seamlessly with both – and with every style in between. Unobtrusive colours and **simple designs** create a harmony of style.

Top left

NATURAL WITH GREY

The natural look can be ultra-modern. By combining a concrete floor with a large blackboard and somewhat austere furnishings, an up-to-the-minute industrial look has been successfully created.

Top right

CLASSICAL

Pale chairs and white walls counterbalance an imposing cupboard of heavily grained wood. In this way, the classical look is kept light and airy.

Bottom left

A NEW WAY WITH LIGHTING

This table stands in the centre of an empty ascetic space. To create interest, wooden chairs with curved backs and slatted seats have been chosen. The lighting solution is novel – instead of overhead lights, a metal standard with three directable spotlights is used.

Bottom right

A LIGHTER SHADE OF WOOD

The dark-coloured wood of this table and chairs has been lightened with a transparent, white wood stain. The timber has then been coated with a clear varnish. Better quality varnishes reduce discoloration of wood by sunlight.

Furnishing fabrics for the natural interior

Left
NATURE INDOORS
Furnishing fabrics in natural
shades, from creamy white
to sand, or tawny to jute.
Restrained patterns are best
suited to this style.

Top and bottom left
OLD AND NEW CROCKERY
Creamy white china goes
well with natural-coloured
furnishings. Look out for odd
pieces that you like at jumble
sales or flea markets. They will
easily combine through colour
to form a complete service.

Centre left
NEW BLADES FOR OLD
Old knives with bone handles
usually have blades that have
oxidized over the years.
If the handle is too good to
throw away, replace the blade
with a new one of stainless
steel. Seek them out in antique
shops specializing in cutlery
and silverware.

Right
**OIL AND VINEGAR
IN FINE BOTTLES**
Part of living life to the full is
eating well, and that includes
using virgin olive oils and
spiced vinegars. Specialist
shops sell many different
varieties of oil and vinegar.

Far right
**SHOP COUNTER
AS DRESSER**
A long shop counter is used
to display a collection of food
covers, jars and other glassware,
including cake stands. Large-
scale counters and display
cabinets can be obtained
through antique dealers.

Living well

The country atmosphere is associated with warmth, sociability and a sense

of security, where you feel at ease amidst furniture and possessions that have

a story to tell. Many collections and **personal bits and pieces** help to create

this atmosphere, whether they are made of glass, earthenware, wicker or

wood. The greatest fun is to be had at jumble sales and markets searching for

that one missing item you have been after for years.

Natural 20

Top left
TWO-COLOURED
Old stair treads are often so worn that it is a good idea to nail new ones on to them. By painting the treads a warm brown instead of white, greater depth is given to the staircase and a link is created with the floor of the landing.

Centre left
MEZZANINE FLOOR
The different levels between bathroom and bedroom are linked by steps.

Bottom left
ROUND AND STRAIGHT
Every line of this staircase is rigidly straight except for the curved supports for the treads. The materials used – wood, metal and concrete – create an industrial-look hallway, which is also natural in style.

Right
MADE TO MEASURE
There was no staircase in this former coach house, so the family designed their own. The stairs are suspended over the void and are made of iroko hardwood treated with oil.

Far right
A DOOR ON THE STAIRS
To prevent all the warmth escaping to the attic, the owners of this home have sawn in half lengthwise an old door left over from rebuilding work. Positioned on the fourth tread of the staircase, the door fits exactly into the small area of ceiling that partially extends over the stairs.

Custom-made, adapted to meet new requirements, painstakingly stripped: unpainted wooden staircases, in which **the wood grain is revealed,** contribute enormously to the overall country atmosphere. The natural, rustic look of untreated timber works particularly well with **white gloss-painted** doors and windows in the hall or on the landing.

A choice
of stairs

NATURAL TREADS
Natural treads are best coated with a special floor varnish that is resistant to wear. If this makes them too slippery, cut grooves at the front of the tread to take small rubber, anti-slip strips, available from builders' merchants. Where the steps are past renovation, new ones can be fitted.

Far left
THE COLOUR OF A FRENCH FARMHOUSE

If you have yet to choose the colours for your bedroom, it is a good idea to base them on the colours in a painting you intend to hang there. What makes this wall so attractive is the way it has been sponged to resemble the external wall of a French farmhouse.

Left
ALTERNATIVE DECOR

This bedroom creates a feeling of modest luxury. The walls are painted off-white and the bed is not a focal point. An unusual chandelier of goose feathers and a glass display cabinet have been chosen to decorate the room instead of works of art on the wall.

Right
NEATLY IN RHYTHM

All the clothes are placed on identical hangers so that everything hangs at the same level, making them easy to find.

For modest luxury

Blue in the bedroom is considered to ensure a **calm, restful and luxurious** atmosphere, and natural colours can have the same effect. A wall emulsioned in beige, combined with bedclothes of cotton and linen, gives the bedroom **a country feel,** or, with the addition of broken white, a **more classical** style. The bedroom should be a place in which you can revive yourself.

Letting in the light

OPENING UP FOR MORE LIGHT

Built-in wardrobes between two bedrooms can be opened up (and the wall removed) if an en suite bedroom is desired. Here, two casement doors have been placed in the wall so that the glass lets in plenty of light. The architrave was made by a timber merchant to match the existing mouldings in the house.

Top left

**A CLASSICAL
WROUGHT-IRON BED**

This modern iron bedframe,
decorated with romantic coils,
is a variation on the antique
bedstead. The little table is
ideal for breakfast in bed.

Top right

SIMPLICITY IS BEAUTIFUL

Natural also means pure –
a theme that is carried through
in this bedroom by a minimum
of decoration. Everything
is kept simple, from the
bedclothes to the doorknobs.

Bottom left

A BRIGHT ATTIC ROOM

An attic room can be made
light and airy by painting the
walls and roof white; this also
helps to avoid the feeling that
the roof is closing in on you.
Insulation material is covered
by painted planking.

Bottom right

**OPEN FIREPLACE
IN THE BEDROOM**

There were at least four
fireplaces in this house. What
could be more romantic? The
tall candlesticks lined up on
the mantelpiece introduce an
elegant touch to an otherwise
cosy and informal room.

Right
NATURAL FLOORS

In an unusual combination
of hard and soft materials,
a **LINOLEUM** border is inset
into a **SISAL** floor-covering.
TILES with an 'antique' glaze
create the appearance of
flagstones but are less porous.
RUSH MATTING is an ancient
material that once kept the
floors of fishermen's homes
warm and is now highly
regarded for its roughly
textured appearance.
OLD WOOD BLOCKS can
be bought from architectural
salvage yards. They look good
laid in patterns. Solid parquet
can also be used.
Simple **FLOOR TILES**, with
a Mediterranean look, are also
suitable for indoors. This
bouclé carpet looks like sisal
but, in fact, is made of
WOOL, combining the soft
texture of wool with the raw
appeal of sisal.
Real **SISAL** can now be found
in a wide range of colours,
including many natural shades.
The colour of **TERRAZZO**
is determined by the colour
of the base concrete and that
of the stone and glass fragments
set into it. Here creamy white,
light yellow and russet
fragments have been used.

Far right
PINE FLOOR

This pine floor was stained
the burnt orange colour of
Oregon pine, not just
because the people who live
here like it, but also to
prevent discoloration by
the sun. The floor was then
varnished for protection.

WOOD COLOUR TO TASTE

Certain timbers are
no longer available
commercially for
environmental reasons,
while others are
prohibitively expensive.
By applying wood stain
to ordinary pine flooring
purchased at the local
DIY store, it is possible
to create a realistic
imitation of reddish-
brown mahogany or red
cherry wood without
spending a great deal
of money.

The warmth of wood, the practicality of tiles, or the combination of both of these properties in linoleum. **Old materials or new**: with a natural interior and neutral furnishings, there are many variations to choose from when it comes to flooring.

Floors with warmth

With the character of the past

Far left
MODERN OAK

The people who live in this house designed their own kitchen in oak, and had a specialist joiner make it up. The combination of oak furniture and a stone floor creates a country atmosphere.

Left
ORIGINAL CUPBOARD

An old storage cupboard can be given a facelift by the addition of new doors, in this case glazed ones.

Top right
TIDIED AWAY

There is masses of space for groceries, crockery and pots and pans in this custom-made, oak kitchen cupboard.

Centre right
NOSTALGIA: A STONEWARE SINK

This kitchen sink made of stone, with its tall mixer tap, is deep enough to take buckets for filling and plant pots for watering. The worktop should overlap the sink slightly to hold it securely in place.

Bottom right
RUSTIC CHARM

A solid timber butcher's block makes a convenient and robust surface for preparing food.

Today's natural-style kitchen combines **the convenience of the present with a nostalgic love of the past.** Modern ingenuity hides behind panel cupboard doors, with beech worktops, a stoneware basin and an original storage cabinet fitted with new glazed doors. The traditional farm-style kitchen, in which the entire family would gather for the evening, **encourages plentiful cooking and appetizing meals to be eaten at leisure.**

Classic cream with beech

PLAIN WHITE TILING
Just like the white tiled walls
at the butcher's, these tiles are
seamless; in other words, they
are laid touching each other
with no grout in between.
This is simple to do, even
for those less skilled at DIY.
The width of the cupboard
doors varies. Only those
hiding the washing machine
and refrigerator were made
to a prescribed size.

Top left
SHOWING OFF

The farmhouse look is created by displaying the dinner service on a dresser. In the past, only the best porcelain was shown off in this way, but even simple, everyday china looks special on open shelves.

Top right
OLD TIMBER

Old timber planks make lovely kitchen cupboard doors and create a country kitchen look. They combine well with the stone floor and worktop. The handy rail in front of the oven is ideal for drying tea towels.

Bottom left
HARMONY WITH COLOUR

The family who live in this house wanted a link between the kitchen and dining-room, so they bought oak from a timber merchant for both the dining-room floor and the kitchen cupboards.

Bottom right
COLLECTING A DINNER SERVICE

It is possible to collect antique dinner services by keeping an eye open at flea markets, auctions, and antique and junk shops. It is a good idea to research the prices your chosen service commands, so that you can spot a real bargain.

Top left
NEW BANISTER

Although the right-hand banister of this staircase was in good repair, the left-hand side and the balusters were replaced by a carpenter, who matched the detailing of the original.

Centre left
TWO INTO ONE

Two built-in cupboards next to each other could be made into one wider wardrobe by removing the wall between them and their shelves. The two old doors are set off by a generous plinth.

Bottom left
OLD BEAMS

A new window has been installed in the roof of a former coach-house to let in more light. The original beams have been sanded and treated with wood stain.

Right
PANELLED DOORS FOR BUILT-IN WARDROBES

Five old doors close off a built-in wardrobe. The depth of the cupboard was determined by the size of the central heating boiler installed inside. The walls are timbered in the same way as the roof.

Far right
A LIGHT AND AIRY ATTIC

Where there was once a small window, a large dormer has been built with French doors. The doors were the starting point of the project and were purchased from an architectural salvage yard. The attic was insulated with mineral wool which was covered with tongue-and-groove boarding rather than plasterboard.

Working in the attic

Those who work regularly **at home** may be able to create a study or workshop in the attic. Many attics are used merely for storage, but there is often masses of wasted space. With built-in cupboards, efficient insulation, a dormer window to let in light and an off-white paint for the timber, the attic can become both an excellent **study or workshop and storage area.**

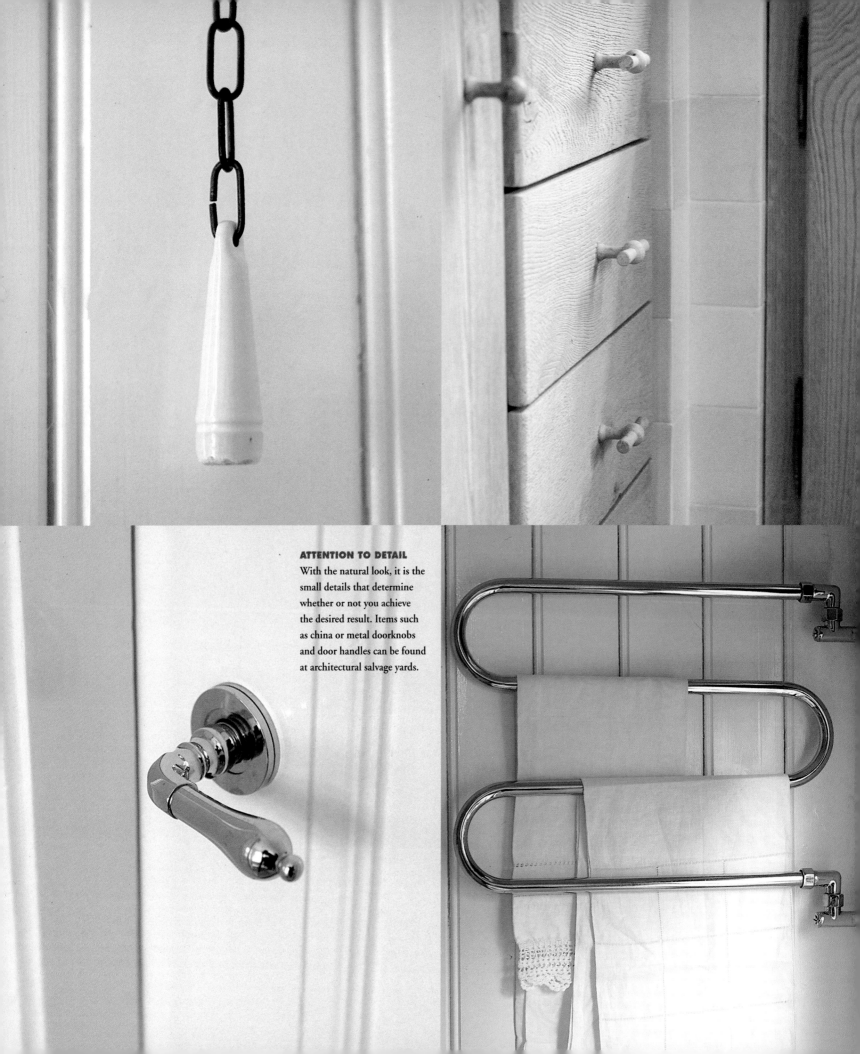

ATTENTION TO DETAIL
With the natural look, it is the
small details that determine
whether or not you achieve
the desired result. Items such
as china or metal doorknobs
and door handles can be found
at architectural salvage yards.

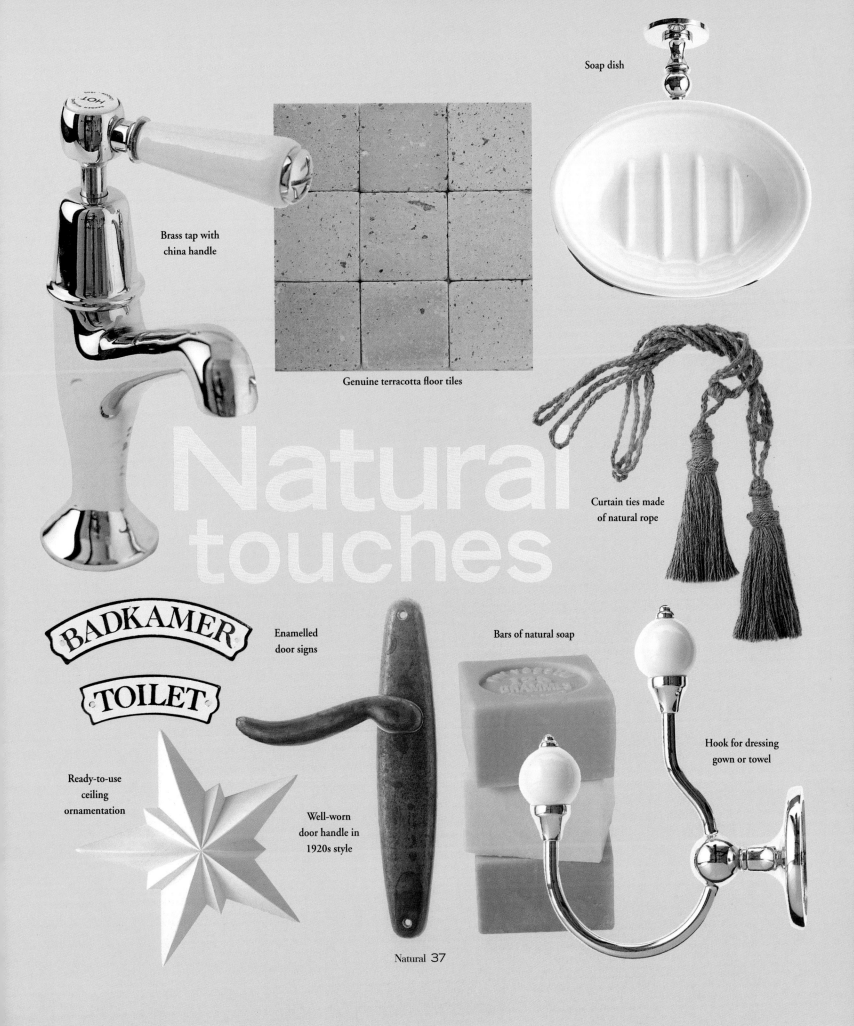

Brass tap with
china handle

Genuine terracotta floor tiles

Soap dish

Curtain ties made
of natural rope

Natural
touches

BADKAMER

TOILET

Enamelled
door signs

Bars of natural soap

Hook for dressing
gown or towel

Ready-to-use
ceiling
ornamentation

Well-worn
door handle in
1920s style

Natural 37

THE RIGHT PLACE
An old bath is best sited with plenty of room around it, although this does mean that the taps will need to be connected to plumbing under the floor. An alternative is to place the bath against a wall, in which case the plumbing can be hidden behind panelling.

EXTERNAL BLIND

The louvre blind is actually fitted between two windows. The inner window can easily be opened without getting in the way of the blind.

Far left centre
NATURAL STONE

Stone does not have to be laid in large rectangular pieces. Used on curved surfaces, it can be surprisingly seductive. The soapstone and travertine marble shown here have similar natural patterning.

Far left bottom
IN STYLE

They look old but are brand new. Various antique-style sockets and light switches can be found to match your chosen style. Special safety regulations apply to electrical wiring for bathrooms.

Left
BATH ON LION'S FEET

A free-standing old bath on lion's feet lends a touch of times past. Ensure that the timber floor is waterproof by sealing the joints and either coating the wood with yacht varnish or impregnating it thoroughly with preservative.

Right
PURE BEAUTY

It is the little details like this delightful metal soap tray hanging over the edge of the bath that give a touch of luxury.

The natural-look bathroom calls out for simplicity, but just **how you interpret simplicity in your plans is entirely up to you.** The bathroom pictured on the left is unmistakably nostalgic, with the original enamel bath complete with lion's feet. By contrast, you can set your bath in a stone surround. Such a bathroom is also natural, but of **modern and uncluttered design.**

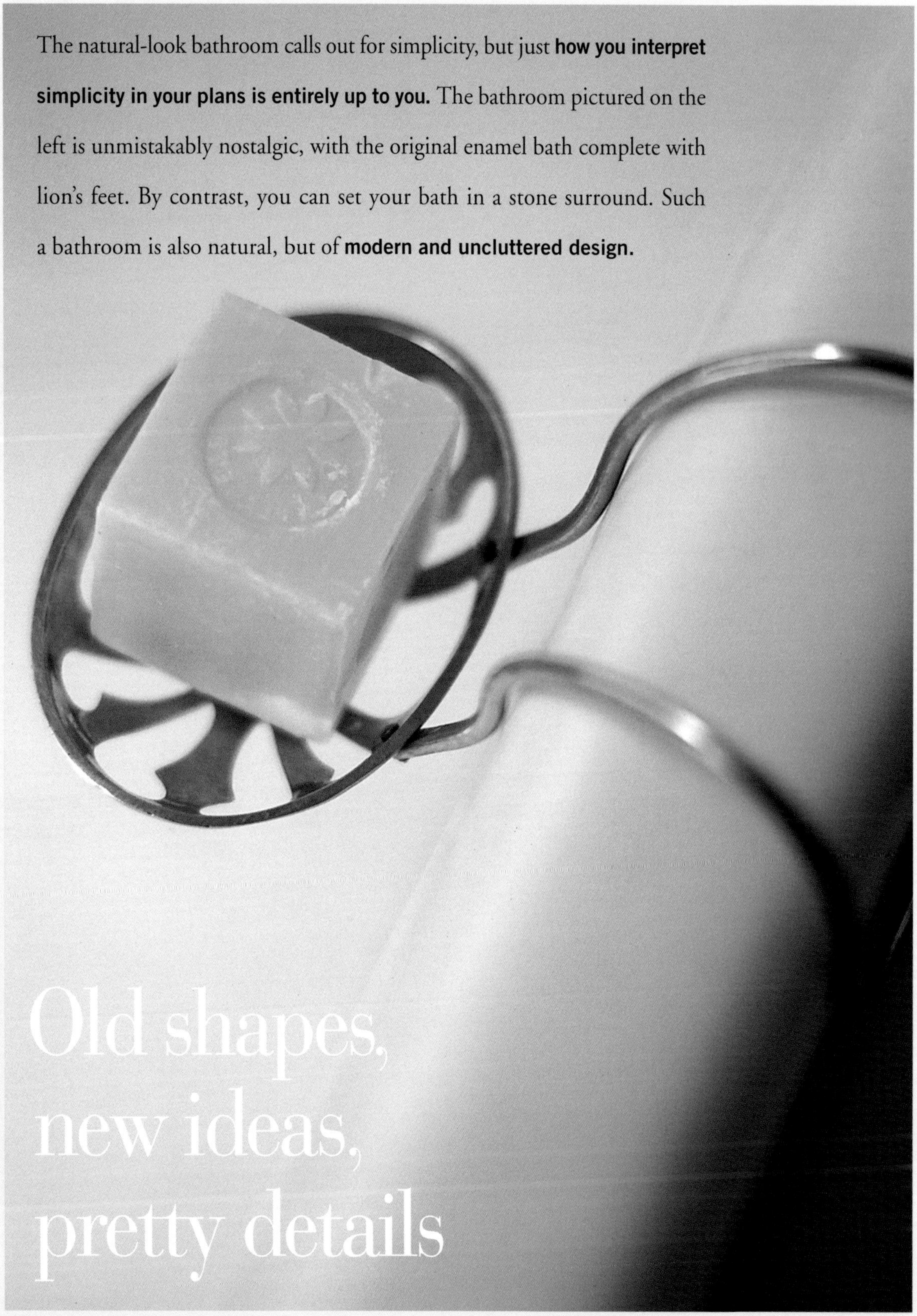

Old shapes,
new ideas,
pretty details

Left
SEPARATE YET TOGETHER
Two individual washbasins
that are not inset make a small
bathroom look bigger. The
shelf above links them together
and provides somewhere to
put all the toiletries. Timber is
fine in the bathroom, provided
it is painted or varnished.

Bottom left
PRETTY AND PRACTICAL
No more will the soap slip
into the basin. A liquid soap
dispenser is also a practical
addition to any bathroom.

Bottom right
**A CLASSIC IN NEW
CLOTHES**
Pedestal washbasins are typical
of bathrooms in older houses,
and modern equivalents are
widely available. The contrast
between the old-fashioned
basin and the modern taps
adds an element of humour.

Right
**OUTWARD OPENING
DOORS**
There are many ways of
creating the illusion of space
in a small bathroom. Glazed
doors that open outwards for
a bathroom with little depth
is just one of them.

The romantic style
of a seaside cottage

Soft Design

Basics are best is the simple philosophy behind the concept of soft design. It combines carefully thought-out design with a sensitive approach to colour and texture, to give a room atmosphere and complement an architectural space. **Soft** is introduced to a room in colours, in curved shapes, and materials that positively invite a tactile response. **Soft** is emphasized through contrasts — matt against glossy, smooth against rough — a theme that can be carried through to the smallest details.

Subtle contrasts soften a pared-down space

Soft colours, soft shapes

2 CONTENTS

Soft Design

Soft Design

**THE COLOUR PALETTE
OF SOFT DESIGN**

These colours are pastel but
not everyday pastel tints.
The addition of a tiny trace
of grey in most of the colours
produces a more sophisticated
effect, away from the 'baby'
pastels of the nursery. Subtlety
is the keyword – the soft green
of a leaf after the first frost,
or the delicate blush of a misty
spring dawn. These hues go
well with plastic and look
good alongside matt metal
or against bleached wood.

TRANSPARENT BUILDING BLOCKS

Instead of a large window in the outside wall of this home, a number of glass blocks have been set into the wall, each resembling a porthole to the outside world. These contribute to the room's tranquil air, together with the brightness and lightness of touch that is the hallmark of soft design. Grey tones contrast with the pretty pastel shades, and light fills the room with an ethereal touch.

Light, bright and spacious

Soft design is happily at home in a newly built house. **Lean lines are mixed with curved shapes** for a modern look that is full of surprises, yet still accessible and personal. This can also be achieved by using combinations of materials, such as steel and glass, plastic and concrete, mellowed by the **warmth of wood.** This spacious look leaves room for light to flood in.

**A NICE TOUCH:
TALLER SKIRTINGS**
The low skirting-board
that is common in newly
built homes can be
extended for an entirely
different effect. Adjust
the height of existing
skirtings by gluing an
additional timber
moulding to them.

Subtle watercolours

Left

THE CLASSICAL WITH SOFT DESIGN

Classical elements work surprisingly well with this style. The light blue of the walls, the gleaming chest of drawers and the 'businesslike' grey sisal floor-covering provide an effective foil for the cream armchair.

Right

CONSIDERED SIMPLICITY

The L-shaped seating area is back in fashion. Everything in this room contributes to the feeling of spaciousness, from the large cushions to the real stone tiles. The design of the coffee table suggests that the inspiration for the room may have been Japanese in origin.

PLANNING THE LIGHTING

For furniture and pictures to be displayed to best effect, the lighting has to be in exactly the right place. The position of your lights should be carefully considered at the building (or rebuilding) stage to avoid having any unsightly cables on show.

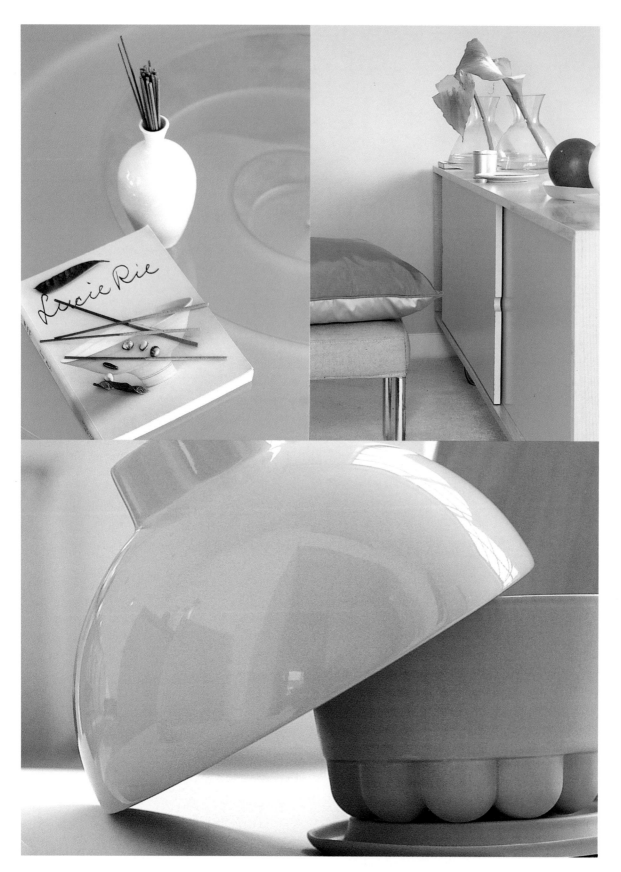

Top left
THE ART OF EXCLUSION
In some ways soft design mirrors Japanese aestheticism. It shares the subtle colours and the minimalist art of knowing what to leave out. But these rounded shapes give new life to the style, making it an interpretation rather than a copy of Eastern principles.

Top right
HARD MATERIALS, DELICATE COLOURS
The cupboard and foot stool are sober and minimalist in design, but the delicate blend of pale blue, lilac and silvery grey colours creates an inviting feel, which is typical of soft design. An important element is repetition of form, shown here by the pair of glass vases containing identical leaves. This simple trick produces a strong, pleasing rhythm.

Bottom
CONTRASTS: GLOSS WITH MATT
Gleaming white china and matt earthenware in a subdued shade of orange act as foils for each other. This juxtaposition of items with different surfaces is a feature of soft design.

THE LOW DRESSER
Curved and rounded shapes, one of the hallmarks of soft design, contrast with the linear dresser on its long, slim legs. This is a reinterpretation of the style of the 1950s.

KOUNELLIS   Gloria Moure

Subtleties of shade for modest luxury

Top left
JAPANESE WAYS
WITH A BLIND

This translucent Japanese
blind is a clever and convenient
solution for covering a roof
window. Held in line with the
awkward angle of the ceiling
by fixtures behind the rods, it
is both practical and attractive.

Centre left
NOSTALGIC SHUTTERS

Shutters are typical of French
houses, traditionally made of
wood or, more recently, metal.
These streamlined accordion
blinds take up very little space.
To create a more Mediterranean
feel, use wooden louvre doors,
available from DIY stores or
builders' merchants.

Bottom left
GLASS BLOCKS: IDEAL
BUILDING MATERIAL

Glass blocks can be used on
their own to pierce walls with
light, or in rows to create a
transparent wall, which also
acts as a window.

Right
ARCHITECTURAL CORNERS

An opening in the wall which
separates the sitting-room
from the landing ensures that
the staircase is not completely
shut off from the room. The
steel banister was custom-made.

Considered details

Soft design includes small architectural details that have been carefully
planned. These are **innovative solutions** that are simultaneously practical and
pleasing to the eye, obvious yet unusual, and the traditional rules of design
are thrown away in the constant search for them. **The strength of this style
lies not in bold gestures but in lightness of touch.**

Top left
USING LIGHT
Steel reflects light while glass allows it to pass through. Plate glass separates the staircase from the landing, bathing it in light, and glass blocks introduce more light from a different source. A subtle interplay of colours is created by the many varying shades of grey.

Top right
FOCUS ON A DOOR
The porthole conjures up images of luxury liners from the 1930s. To solve the rather awkward problem of a very wide doorway, the hinges have been mounted on the top and bottom of the door roughly two-thirds along its width. When it is open, the door then takes up no more room than a normal-sized door.

Bottom left
SYMMETRY AND COLOUR
By glazing all the doors in this home, a continuity of style has been created. The doors are divided vertically into three equal sections, establishing a rhythm throughout the house.

Bottom right
ELEGANT SIMPLICITY
Soft green cupboard doors by Philippe Starck, extending from floor to ceiling, form a cupboard wall entirely in keeping with soft design. The simplicity of the design draws attention to the small detail of the door handles. The chairs, also designed by Starck, are simple self-assembly affairs of wood and plastic.

LESS IS MORE

This bedroom has everything
it needs – no more, no less.
The slim lines of the 1950s-
style lamp and small table
make them look almost
weightless, an illusion that
is echoed in the bed, which
seems to float on air because
the legs are recessed out of
sight. The concrete floor
underscores the simplicity.

**RESTFUL, SIMPLE
COLOUR SCHEMES**

For a restful bedroom,
use the same colour for
the floor and the walls.
Hold paint samples
against the wall and
on the floor to choose
the colour in the room's
ambient light. Use the
same samples to choose
the floor-covering.

Homeliness without excess is
the secret here. Lavender blue
is well proven as a restful
colour for the bedroom, and,
combined with butter yellow
and off-white, it creates a soft
mood which is accentuated
by the light filtering through
the translucent curtains. The
lamps, cupboard and plain
bedding are kept as simple as
possible, and the squared-off
piles of pillows and bedclothes
provide a visual rhythm.

Tranquil simplicity

The bedroom can be **furnished minimally** in the soft design style. The only

apparent theme here is simplicity, but a delicate mood is created by the

choice and combination of elements, such as the slim lines of the table and

lamps and the plump forms of the pillows and bed. The coolness of soft

design makes a bedroom an **oasis of tranquillity**.

Fabrics to suit the soft design mood

SUBDUED TINTS
Unobtrusive shades, pastel watercolours and delicate designs are best suited to the rounded forms of soft design.

Businesslike with a lighter touch

Far left
A DESIGN EVERGREEN
The butterfly chair has stood the test of time. The slender legs (fitted with wheels, if required) and delicate shape lend themselves to soft design.

Left
WOOD IS HONEST AND WARM
Without the natural elements of the wooden sideboard and gourds, the stone and glass table would create an entirely different effect. Notice, too, the restful colour combination of the warm-toned wood and the lilac-grey table base with its green plate glass top.

Top right
VERTICAL BOOKCASE
This simple, made-to-measure ladder on wheels is practical and also a work of art.

Bottom right
KITCHEN ISLAND UNIT
A modern solution to the kitchen table, this island unit, constructed from wood blocks, has everything: double sink, cooking hob and drawers with recessed handles. The wall cupboards share the simple, restrained lines of this style.

Now that increasing numbers of people work at home, the design of the workspace is acquiring a **lighter touch**. Soft design strives for feather-light answers that are both aesthetic and practical. Cupboards with masses of storage space replace filing cabinets, and industrial materials, such as metal tubing, are **combined with wood** to provide the essential ingredient of warmth. Finally, desk furniture is arranged to provide a pleasing visual rhythm.

Left
SHAPED TO FIT

The shape of the heated towel rail echoes the space, and the shiny chrome provides an eye-catching contrast with the tiles. Small mosaics are easier to work with than larger ones if the bathroom's design includes unusual or difficult shapes.

Right
SOFT DESIGN IS INNOVATIVE

Round shapes suit a bathroom well. They are pleasing to the eye, and the absence of sharp corners and angles makes the room that much easier to keep clean and safer to use.

UNDER-FLOOR HEATING SAVES SPACE

The chrome towel rail is intended to dry towels, so some other source of heating is also needed. Under-floor heating is comfortable and completely invisible.

Even when the rest of the house is furnished and decorated in a different style, soft design is perfect for the bathroom. **The combination of chrome and ceramics with glass mosaic** produces architectural details and gently curved

The bathroom

shapes that look as if they were specially intended for bathrooms. Small details can work very effectively in these circumstances. The result is a bathroom made for lengthy relaxation.

Top left
BARGAIN LUXURY

Luxury need not be expensive. Face creams, bath foam and shampoos come in lovely pastel colours and are often packaged in attractive bottles. They are a cheap way of adding a touch of luxury to your bathroom.

Centre left
THE STYLE OF A SMART HOTEL

Attractive details work even better in simple surroundings. Take this into account when working out your budget. A small, quality item, like this toothbrush mug and holder, make you feel as if you are staying in a first-class hotel, and may give more pleasure than expensive floor tiles.

Bottom left
PARTITION WALLS: USEFUL AND ATTRACTIVE

Partition walls in the bathroom can conceal pipework and also function as part of a shower cubicle or shower screen. Here, a shower is fitted over the bath.

Right
EXTRA LARGE SHOWER-HEADS

Shower-heads are available in many different sizes. Check with a plumber that the water pressure will be sufficient for the type you prefer.

The glass door has a natural green tinge. Such subtle shades can be borne in mind when planning the colour scheme for your bathroom. Thermostatic taps are very useful because the water comes out at a predetermined temperature.

FINISHING TOUCH: EDGE PROFILES

Discoloured edging strips around bath and basin should be replaced with mildew-resistant products. Sharp corners formed by tiles set at right angles to each other can be rounded off with special metal edging profiles. Metal profiles can be tiled in the same way as ceramic strips, and the smoother finish on shower or bath looks much smarter

The power of simplicity

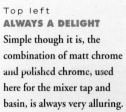

Top left
ALWAYS A DELIGHT
Simple though it is, the combination of matt chrome and polished chrome, used here for the mixer tap and basin, is always very alluring.

Top right
NEW LAMPS
The choice of suitable lighting has an amazing effect. A small, well-designed lamp highlights the other accessories.

Bottom left
STYLE SETTERS, OLD AND NEW
Taps can be found in futuristic modern designs or as replicas of timeless classics. Whatever you choose will set the style of the bathroom. For those seeking a mood of times past, there is ample choice at architectural salvage yards.

Bottom right
PLANNED TO THE SMALLEST DETAIL
The choice of handles and knobs may seem obvious but they are usually the result of careful consideration. These handles echo the bowed shape of the drawer.

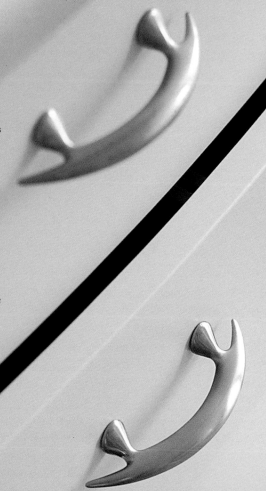

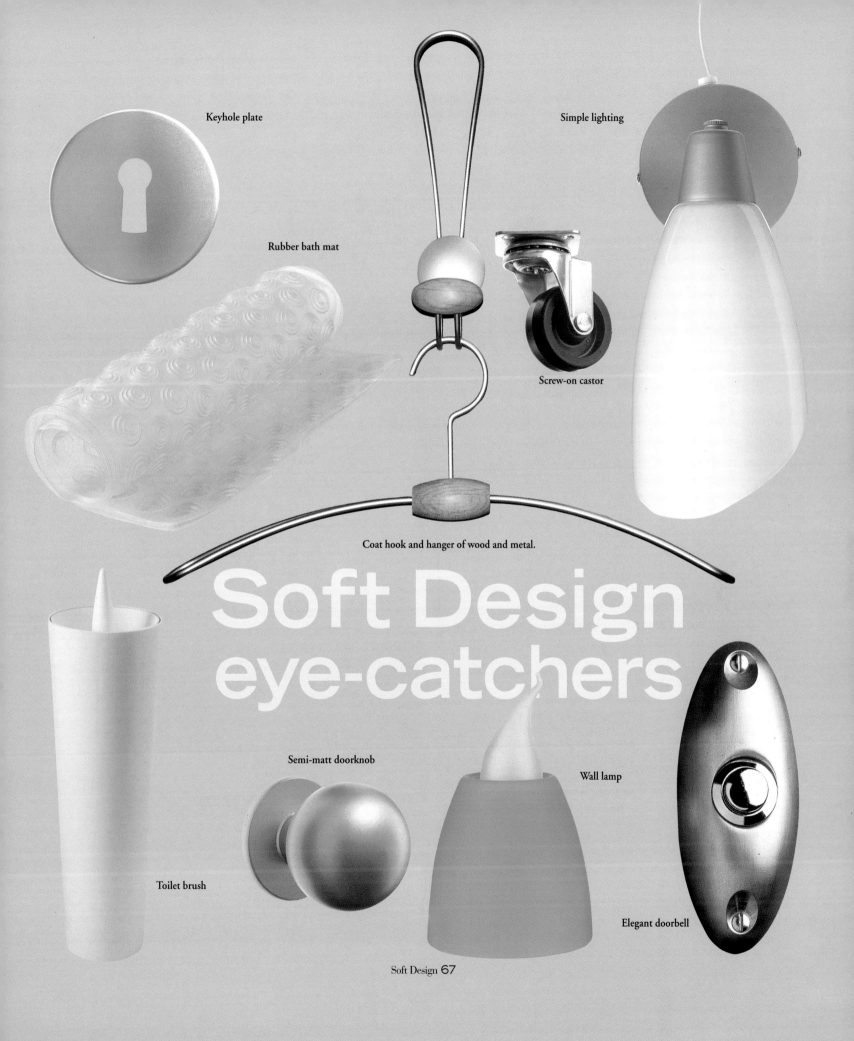

Keyhole plate

Simple lighting

Rubber bath mat

Screw-on castor

Coat hook and hanger of wood and metal.

Soft Design
eye-catchers

Semi-matt doorknob

Wall lamp

Toilet brush

Elegant doorbell

Top left
BLOCK-FORM STAIRS

Stairs that are not open plan usually have treads that slightly overshoot the risers. Although this might seem a small detail, the absence of such an overlap is very noticeable in this flight of stairs, which has the rather unusual appearance of blocks piled on top of one another.

Centre left
STAIRS ON LEGS

This close-up of the picture below shows how the bottom of the stairway is supported just off the ground, so that it appears to float. The light and airy effect is increased by the way in which the metal tube disappears into the wood to reappear beneath.

Bottom left
SPATIAL DISCOVERY

This is an example of working within existing constraints: as there was only limited room for the staircase opening, it was given a curved shape. The stairs were constructed from wood similar to that of the floor, which was laid in a herring-bone pattern.

Right
SIMPLICITY IN STYLE

No extraneous detail is allowed in this staircase: there is just one support and cantilevered treads. The combination of black and white and metal is all that is needed to create the desired mood. On the landing, painted a serene white, there is the one detail: an unusual chair made out of cardboard.

TRICKS WITH STAIRS
Stairs that run between two walls are normally fixed at both sides. Here, a small gap has been left on one side, giving the impression of a very lightweight structure.

Architectural thinking

An architect once said that a house without stairs was a wasted opportunity. Indeed, **stairs can be breathtaking** and a wonderful addition to the spaces they join. Something wonderful can be achieved by **linking the design to the surroundings** and by selecting materials in keeping with the style of the house, whether the stairs are open plan or enclosed.

COMBINATION OF SHAPES
An optimum combination of stairs, banister and stairwell. The family who live here had the banisters specially made by a firm that manufactures yacht masts and spars.

There are certain guidelines for floors in soft design: **light-coloured woods** can be used to form **an attractive foil** to the more restrained elements of the style, and both sisal, **in tints of grey,** or carpet with a short pile, can be used to the same effect. Other options for flooring within this style are painted concrete, quarry tiles, mosaic and linoleum. Consider colours that mimic **gentle washes of watercolour,** such as silvery grey, sea green or very light blue.

Soft design floors

Left
UNLIMITED DESIGN POTENTIAL

Glass and ceramic mosaic tiles lend themselves to fabulous designs in a huge range of colourways. To strengthen the effect of the mosaic floor and to ensure that nothing detracts from it, the skirting-board can be painted to match the wall.

Right

CARPET with a very short, close pile, makes an ideal floor-covering for soft design. **LINOLEUM** is available in a range of colours and patterns. **TILES** look particularly good laid in rows. These are in slightly grey-tinged pastels, which resemble watercolours. **MOSAIC** suits any style. In soft design, shades with light colour washes are preferred for the softer look they create. **KNOBBED RUBBER** flooring in grey creates an eye-catching, almost industrial look. **CARPET** in soft, pale colours combines well with metal and slender modern furniture. **LAMINATE** is available in many colours and designs, including the popular wood finishes, such as beech, which work well with soft design. **STONE FLOORS** complement soft forms and furnishings, and wooden cupboards. The choice available, from terrazzo to coloured concrete, is huge.

DELINEATING WITH FLOOR PATTERNS
One space can be sub-divided into separate function areas, for example, to indicate the sitting and dining areas of a dual-purpose room, by using different flooring materials or a change of pattern. A sense of partition can also be given by creating a border around the chosen space. Do this only when you are certain what furniture is to be positioned where in the room.

Chairs naturally belong around a table but they need not be of the same design # Around the table

or material. In fact, it is a good idea to **choose chairs that are of a completely**

different material from the table – glass, perhaps, with wood, or plastic with

metal. You can also successfully **combine round forms with rectangular.**

To finish, use a sleek lamp to direct light on to the table.

PLAYING WITH CONTRASTS

These Philippe Starck chairs are made of thin plastic yet have the shape and bulk of upholstered chairs. The plate glass tabletop appears fragile compared with the massive base. The design is unadorned so that nothing detracts from its strong statement.

Top left
KITCHEN WITH A SITTING-ROOM FEEL

The kitchen has been installed in a low-ceilinged attic. On one side there is a sliding door and facing it the worktop, which is made from grey terrazzo without any added colour. The aim was to achieve a sitting-room effect, with the worktop acting as a dresser.

Top right
NEW LOOK FOR THE 1950S

Scandinavian furniture designs from the 1950s are once again in vogue. Their best features are the slender legs and flowing lines with little embellishment. The table is made of plastic as opposed to wood, so that the attractive shapes of the chairs are not overshadowed.

Bottom left
INDOOR PATIO

The sense of relaxing on a patio with a cup of coffee and a sandwich or snack can be created indoors with a small table and some chairs. Add a book or newspaper, and the illusion is complete.

Bottom right
OPEN-PLAN KITCHEN

The solid-looking wooden table forms a bridge between the kitchen and sitting-room. As a cooker hood over the hob would have marred the lines of the kitchen design, an extractor unit was fitted out of sight under the worktop.

MARBLE SURFACES
Marble can be 'tumbled' or 'polished': polishing produces a glossier effect whilst tumbling gives a denser surface which is easier to keep clean. Marble has to be cut to size with great accuracy, and a cardboard template is essential to show the exact placing of power points, for example.

A new look at cooking

Soft design in the kitchen is a **modern interior style** that takes into account your daily requirements, such as producing tasty and nourishing meals with quality ingredients in the minimum amount of time. These needs are taken care of with **practical kitchen design**, strategically placed appliances and easy-to-clean worktops. The style incorporates stainless steel surfaces, warm beechwood units, simple handles and useful racks, and demonstrates how **the functional and the aesthetic can be harmoniously combined.**

Far left
PRACTICAL AND AESTHETIC

The free-standing island unit is of double depth and has back-to-back cupboard space. Openings at the tops of the doors replace handles.

Left
THE KITCHEN/LIVING-ROOM

Stainless steel, marble, and streamlined cupboard doors: there is something of the atmosphere of a professional restaurant about this kitchen. At the same time, the natural tiled floor, classic white crockery and rounded corners of the unit fronts clearly show that it is a room designed with the whole family in mind.

Above right
THE ALL-MARBLE KITCHEN

The entire back wall of the dresser unit consists of a large marble slab. Even the shelving, fixed in place from behind, is made of the same cool material.

Centre right
A STYLISH SOLUTION

In a flexible kitchen layout, deciding where to hang tea towels can be something of a problem. Here, simple white tea towels are knotted to a rail: they look decorative as well as being close to hand.

Below right
THE RESTAURANT TOUCH

Well-designed kitchen utensils, containers, dispensers and tea towels are attractively arranged in a practical and accessible display. Plain white china or traditional designs would look equally good in this setting.

Top left
LIGHT-HEARTED TOUCHES

Refrigerators and cookers influenced by American design of the 1960s are light-hearted introductions to the kitchen. The porthole in the oven door is a perfect soft design feature.

Centre left
TRANSPARENT AND ROUNDED

Small details lend themselves to an entirely novel approach such as these transparent knobs.

Bottom left
FLOATING KITCHEN UNIT

This kitchen unit appears to float because its plinth has been placed far back out of sight. The draining-board finishes flush with the cupboard doors to provide neat, soft lines.

Right
GRAPHIC EFFECT

The division of cupboard doors and kitchen appliances creates an almost graphic pattern. Note where the door handles have been positioned, so that they form an attractive line alongside the oven.

LET THE KITCHEN UNIT FLOAT

As shown on the left, a kitchen unit can appear to float in the air when its plinth is set back. This also allows you to stand closer to the unit, making it easier to reach across, which is particularly important if you have chosen a deep worktop.

Completely in style: 'soft' shapes

IN ITALIAN STYLE
Curved shapes juxtaposed
with formality is typical of
Italian design. In this kitchen,
the properties of the materials
used have been fully exploited,
as illustrated by the rounded
metal edge of the worktop.

Handling details

Doorknobs and handles are more abundant in the kitchen than anywhere else in the home and they therefore deserve special consideration. The type you choose will stamp its style on a cupboard door and contribute to the overall mood you wish to create. Whether classic or modern, formal or light-hearted, suitable knobs and handles for the soft design look often include rounded features, which are **pleasing to touch** and work harmoniously with the overall design.

**DOOR HANDLES
MAKE THE KITCHEN**
An enormous
range of handles and
knobs for kitchen
cupboards and drawers
can be bought from
specialist suppliers
as well as DIY stores.
These pictures illustrate
just a few of the
different designs and
materials available.

CHAPTER 3

New Classical

A modern look at tradition

The classical approach to interior design for the home has always been about quality and form. The new classical style places this within a fresh framework. The colour palette of **taupe, greyish-brown and the patina of worn silver** works beautifully with dark wood and subtle ornamentation, reminiscent of the colonial style. It is this combination of clean lines, simple shapes and neutral colours, lifted by decorative detail, that results in a sophisticated style with echoes of an elegant French home or New York apartment: **a timeless style rejuvenated.**

New Classical

Subtle colours and decorative details

3 CONTENTS

DE PSALMEN

Boudewijn Büch | Geestgrond

New Classical

**THE NEW CLASSICAL
COLOUR PALETTE**

Classical colours range from
creamy white, through the
natural colours of grey, brown
and taupe, on to spicy ginger
and cinnamon, finishing with
the deepest midnight blue.
Sophisticated and dramatic,
these colours look superb with
antique furniture, aged gold
leaf and matt silvery metal.

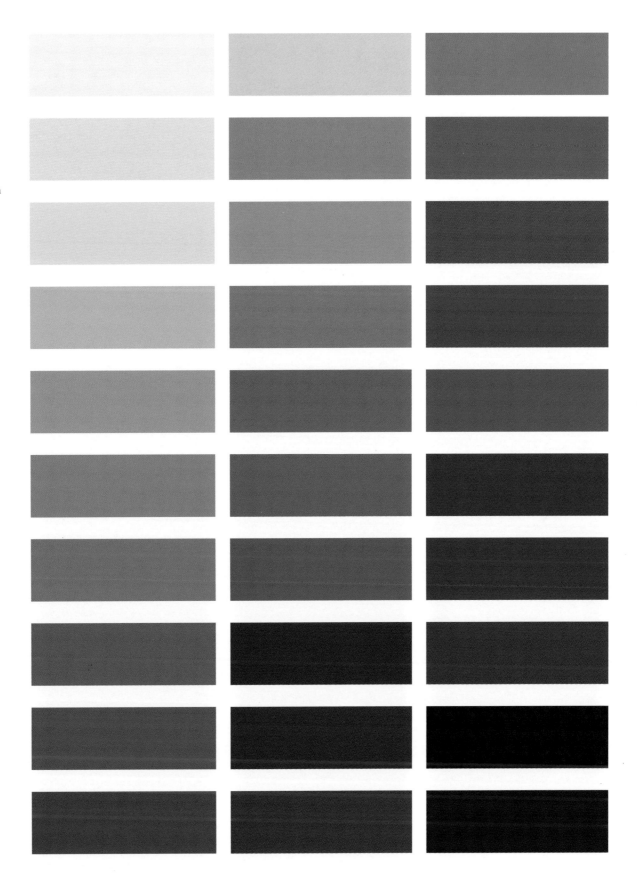

New Classical

Divide the space differently

New times call for new ideas. How you decide to divide up the space in your home should be determined by your lifestyle rather than by tradition. Furnishings in the classical style have great potential because they have the same **strong presence** even when they are arranged in completely new ways.

**MAKING THE MOST
OF A SMALL SPACE**
When not in use, the dining
table and sofa butt up to each
other, and are placed centrally
in the room so as not to take
up circulation space. The dining
chairs are covered with Indian
cotton to blend with the sofa.

Top left
ROOM FOR DESIGN

The owners of this home
painted the larch floor with
antique pine stain and made
3mm (1/8in) grooves between
the floorboards with a router.
The custom-made cupboard
behind the armchair has panels
of perforated metal which veil
the music system, television
and stationery files.

Top right
STATELY AND STYLISH

A fine entrance: the hallway
links the kitchen and sitting-
room. The chairs, upholstered
in off-white canvas, provide an
attractive focal point.

Below
MULTICULTURAL

These simple armchairs are
upholstered in a suede-effect
fabric, which gives them
a lived-in look. Traditional
shields from New Guinea,
in complementary shades of
brown, provide an exotic touch.

Right
LIVING AROUND THE FIRE

An open hearth is the dominant
feature in this room, and the
seating has been loosely arranged
around it. In such a setting,
occasional tables – or in this
case a lidded basket – are a
better design solution than one
central coffee table, resulting
in far more circulation space.

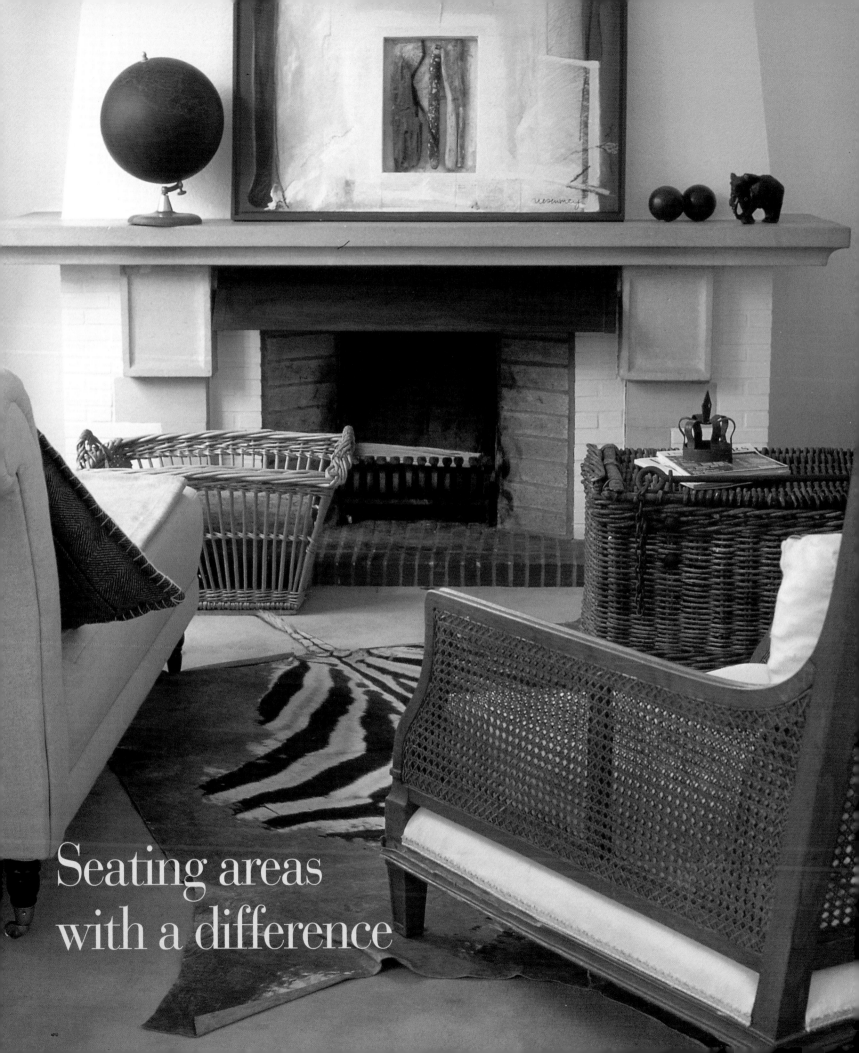

Seating areas
with a difference

The finest furnishing fabrics

FABRICS FULL OF TRADITION
In the new classical style, warm-coloured fabrics offset woods of different tones. Cream and golden shades against the sober colours of dark wood and pottery have a traditional feel.

FIREPROOF BRICKS

The brick fireplace was
recently added to the front
of a chimney consisting of
twin-piped flues. Fireproof
bricks were used to create
a new fireback and surround.

Top right
**MANTELPIECE OF
SANDSTONE**

The warm, rich tones of this
sandstone mantelpiece are
offset by the cool lavender
blue walls and the golden hues
of the wooden floor, gilded
mirror frame and armchair.

Below
**ADDING SUNNY ORANGE
TO THE PALETTE**

The natural stone mantelpiece
surrounding this fireplace is set
against a wall painted in a warm
earth colour, which gives depth
to the grey. Coarse woven mats
suit the colonial look of the
furnishings in shades of brown,
sand and ivory. Two wooden
armchairs have been placed on
the other side of the coffee table
instead of a second sofa. These
are easier to move close to the
fire on cold winter evenings.

Around the hearth

HOW TO USE A LARGE FIRE SURROUND
The size of a fireplace needs to be in proportion to the diameter of the chimney to ensure that the fire draws properly. Where the chimney is small, a large fire surround can still be used if the opening to the fireplace is reduced, as shown here.

STAYING IN PROPORTION
The fireplace should determine the size and scale of furniture in a room, which needs to be in proportion to complement it. The opening to this fireplace has been reduced but it retains the symmetry of its surround.

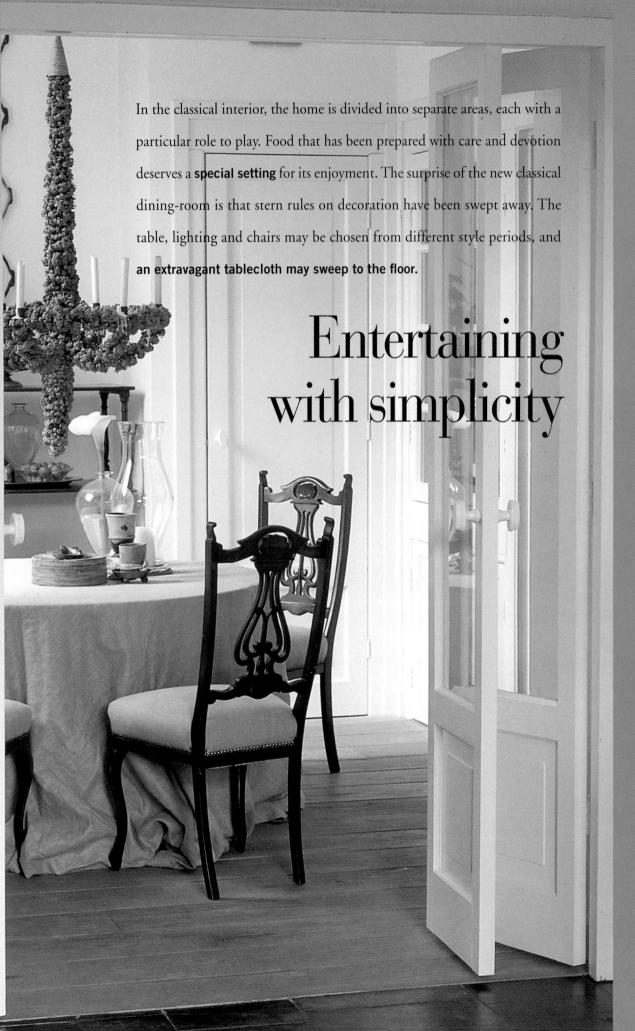

In the classical interior, the home is divided into separate areas, each with a particular role to play. Food that has been prepared with care and devotion deserves a **special setting** for its enjoyment. The surprise of the new classical dining-room is that stern rules on decoration have been swept away. The table, lighting and chairs may be chosen from different style periods, and **an extravagant tablecloth may sweep to the floor.**

Entertaining with simplicity

Left
COMBINING STYLES
At first glance this dining area appears to be in the classical style, but closer examination reveals that it is a mixture of styles from different periods. The chairs are from the turn of the century, and the floor is of oak boarding. The chandelier, a feature of the classical style, is given an up-to-date look.

Right
COLLECTING CHINA
This creamy white china has been collected from several discontinued lines to make an inexpensive dinner service.

Far right top
THE UTILITY LOOK SOFTENED
Modern design can be combined with the classical room. Plastic chairs are given a classical look by the addition of ready-made cream slip-on covers.

Far right bottom
SERVING AS A SIDEBOARD
A corner of the dining area has been found for this small table, which acts as a sideboard, leaving everything within reach of the dining table. The white, antique dinner service is the perfect foil for the colourful still-life in its gilded frame.

A COLOUR EXPERT
Since colour is such an important factor in the decoration and furnishing of your home, it may be wise to seek the help of a professional colour expert. These are usually people with artistic or architectural training who work closely with you to suggest colour combinations that suit your own preferences and style.

travigne 1881

**FROM LINEN CHEST TO
WINE STORE DOOR**
Old furniture can sometimes
be adapted for a new role.
Here the lid of an old linen
chest has been put to use as a
door for a wine store. The chalk
on the string is used to write
notes on the wines. The made-
to-measure table incorporates
a useful slide-out section.

THEATRICAL EFFECT

The deep purple of the wall is an unusual but effective choice for a background against which to hang these gilt-framed pictures. Every evening, the candles are lit in the candle-holders mounted under the pictures; these were all found at flea markets and junk shops. The table is a masterpiece of craftsmanship and subtle design.

HARMONY BETWEEN PAINTINGS AND THEIR BACKGROUND

Art collectors and galleries used to base the background against which paintings were hung upon the tonality of the paintings. A wall filled with works of art in the home can be similarly treated. Little other decoration is required in such a room.

Simple purple and gold

REPLICA DOOR FURNITURE
The handle and lock on this cloakroom door are stylish replicas of an older design.

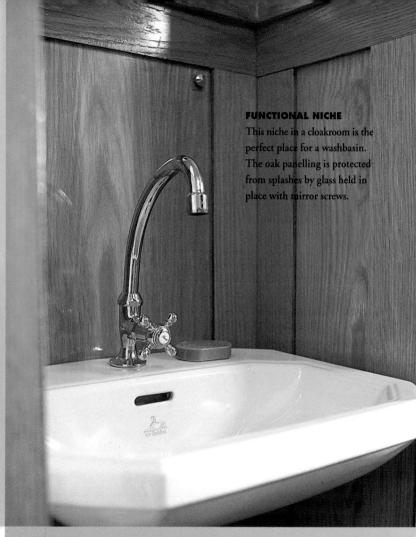

FUNCTIONAL NICHE
This niche in a cloakroom is the perfect place for a washbasin. The oak panelling is protected from splashes by glass held in place with mirror screws.

CHROMED BRASS
Brackets such as this one, used here to support a banister, can be found in shops selling curtain rods and accessories.

BIRDS AS DECORATION
This detail from a door panel shows how attractive carved ornamentation can be. New architectural ornaments are available in a wide range of elements, from swags to single flowers, from which you can create your own design.

BACK AGAIN: WOODEN ORNAMENTATION
Plaster ornaments for ceilings have long been popular, while old door panels were often decorated with wooden designs. Now these are back in vogue, pressed out of wood pulp. They are also excellent for decorating mirror frames.

Made-to-measure
picture frames

Chandelier drops

Gilded ornamental bracket

Curtain rods with
metal finials

Balustrade finial

Classical
details

Door spy-grille

Panels for built-in radiators

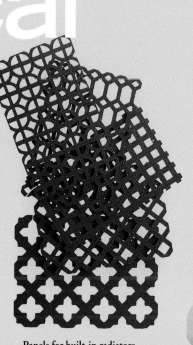

Top left
FOR SHOW

Highly polished wooden storage containers made from tropical hardwood gleam against the light background of a botanical painting. Objects displayed for pure enjoyment can look equally attractive whether grouped together or arranged singly.

Centre left
RHYTHM ON THE WALL

Traditional art from Africa complements the new classical style. The intrinsic value of this collection is enhanced by the rhythmic way in which it is displayed, making it even more eye-catching.

Bottom left
BLACK AND WHITE

Snapshots, prints, engravings and old maps, all yellowing with age, tell their own story.

Right
SIMPLE IS BEST

Floral displays with an oriental feel are most beautiful when kept simple. This jar contains just two arum lily stems.

In the new classical style, **an exotic atmosphere** is created not only through decoration but also through the display of artefacts. Some pieces may be

From distant lands

unique objets d'art, others amusing memorabilia, such as candlesticks with 'leopard' markings, proving that distant lands are not so very far away.

Examples of classical taste are to be found at every point of the compass.

BOXING-IN
Radiators can be boxed in with a decorative wooden grille, so that they blend in with your chosen decor.

OUT OF SIGHT
Many practical items work well with the new classical style, but modern steel radiators are best kept hidden. Here warm oak was used to blend with the rich colours of the room and to form a deeper window sill.

Polished wood and decorative ornaments

The staircase used to be an **introduction to the style of the home.** They were wide and often an example of the craftsmanship of their builder, expressed in curlicues and other ornamentation. The loveliest staircases are often those made of wrought-iron or with turned wood balusters. **Natural wood that has been fashioned with care and worked to a soft shine is beautiful,** even when it is brand new.

Left
HARMONY IN COLOUR
The finely detailed balusters alone make this staircase attractive. If you live in an upstairs apartment, it is best to carpet the stairs, otherwise your neighbours will hear every single footstep. For a truly classical look, carpet only the treads.

Right
CLASSICAL BUT NEW
New stairs can be given an authentic classical look. High gloss varnished wood, with no ornamentation or embellishment other than its natural grain, plus wrought-iron banisters with a flourish of curlicues, provide a rich but contemporary look.

Far right top
STAIR RUNNER
A border has been cut out of this stair carpet and replaced with a contrasting strip to make the carpet look like a made-to-measure runner.

Far right bottom
THE OLDER THE BETTER
The colour of this oak staircase has deepened with the passing of time. The elegant balusters have an almost 'flattened' appearance, helping to create a light and airy stairway.

CONSTRUCTION OF SPECIAL STAIRCASES
Bespoke staircases can be made to suit your requirements by craftsmen or specialist companies.

Modern design with a classical style

There are a number of new techniques and treatments for **natural materials such as stone or marble, slate or wood** that will create a classical look in the bathroom. Here curved shapes and pastel grey mosaic tiles combine the **grandeur of the past** with today's simplicity of style.

Top left
EXOTIC INFLUENCES
The blue and gold patterned tiles in this bathroom evoke the opulent palaces of the Moors.

Top right
CLASSICAL MATERIALS, MODERN DESIGN
Although this bathroom derives its classical ambience from the use of traditional materials, its modern design ensures a fresh elegance. The washbasin is set in a wafer-thin black marble surround, with a gently curving shape.

Bottom left
PLAIN AND SIMPLE
Plain wooden panelling has been used in a small cloakroom to enormous effect. This corner is full of classical details: the niche with its basin, mirror, pendant lamp and glass shelf.

Bottom right
THE CHARM OF WELL-USED MATERIALS
This ancient marble basin was found piled with every sort of object during a visit to an architectural salvage yard. As well as leaving the peeling paint on the basin, no attempt has been made to restore the mirror. Signs of ageing can be charming, especially when the objects are of good quality.

NEW MATERIALS

The rigid lines of stone can
be imitated with a modern
material such as Corian, which
can be worked into any shape.
This solid Corian washbasin
and surround is backed by
a mirror of the same width.

PRESENT-DAY COMFORT

If the budget will run to it,
why not invest in a spa bath
with bubble jets? Your electrical
system may require adaptation
for this, and do not forget that
there are strict regulations for
electricity in bathrooms.

THE RIGHT TAPS

When choosing taps you
should consider the style of
your washbasin or vanity unit.
Make sure there is sufficient
room behind the basin for the
taps to be turned on and off.
Tall taps require deep basins
or the jet is likely to splash
onto the walls and floors.

TRUE SIMPLICITY

For this bathroom an
unconventional approach has
been taken with washbasins
that give the appearance of
two bowls sitting on a table.
The simple wall-mounted taps
complement them perfectly.

Classical and modern in stylish sobriety

BETTER THAN STANDARD
There are standard shapes and sizes for everything in the bathroom, but perhaps a longer or deeper bath would suit you better. The same might be true of the shower. Instead of a standard shower tray you could have one made to measure in non-slip tiles or terrazzo.

It is not just the furniture that determines
the overall look of a room: the walls, curtains,
ceiling and floor all play very important
roles. With the classical interior, the floor
can immediately set the tone of a room,
even before a single chair has been put in
place. Wood, brick and ceramic are natural
and traditional choices that will lend an air
of history and authority to any room.

A manor-house floor in your home

**BROAD PLANKS FOR
A PERIOD LOOK**

The larch wood floor has been treated with antique pine wood stain and the gaps between the floorboards made intentionally wide to enhance the period effect. Pre-war styling has influenced the furniture design.

TERRACOTTA TILES give the air of a farmhouse kitchen but have the advantage in a bathroom of being non-slip.
SMALL MOSAIC TILES are versatile and can be laid in almost any pattern you choose. Their use in bathrooms dates back to Roman times.
PARQUET is floor-covering with a historical look. In order to achieve the manor-house style, lay a darker inset border.
STONE FLOORS can be given a shiny finish using oil but they look equally attractive when left with a matt finish.
QUARRY TILES decorated with colourful patterns are now widely available.
MOSAICS can be laid quickly and easily to fit any area. If the floor is not a true rectangle or square, the edges can be laid piece by piece. Ceramic mosaic tiles, which are less well known, look most attractive laid in an irregular pattern.
WOOD can also be used in wet areas, thanks to modern waterproofing treatments.
TERRAZZO can be broken up with borders of glass mosaic. The two materials are polished to form a smooth surface.

**LOOKING AFTER
NATURAL FLOORING**
Oils and waxes are the best products to use to take care of wooden or stone floors. Always use natural oils, such as linseed, or blends of oils derived from plants.

PERFECT DRAWER
The wooden chests of drawers
that were once a common
feature of lawyers' offices make
a stylish and practical addition
to a study or workroom.

Bottom left
OLD AND NEW TOGETHER
Although the colour of the
wood gives this cupboard
a classical look, the rounded
metal handles and the way in
which the doors open bring
it completely up to date.

Bottom right
**FLOOR-TO-CEILING
DOORS**
Both the wardrobe unit and
the floor have been made from
pale beech. Everything here
is understated, including the
hole pulls for handles. In a box
room or small bedroom, this
unit could be made into a walk-
in wardrobe with a mirror, to
make the room seem larger.

Right
SYMMETRY WITH LINES
The symmetry of the doors and
drawer fronts gives a classical
appearance. Pale birch and a
slightly darker hardwood have
been used together.

Classical style for cupboards

There never seems to be enough cupboard space. Try to make existing cupboards part of the **decorative elements** of your home. Perhaps you can find an interesting example with a history from an antique or junk shop. Alternatively, you may prefer cupboards that are unique for a different reason, because they are custom-made. If they are of the right design, these cupboards will **form an intrinsic part of the style of the room.**

METALLIC PAINT FOR AN EXTRA DIMENSION

Furniture and accessories can be made to look rather special with metallic paint. Most well-known manufacturers produce their own metallic paints, but for small details, modeller's paints can be used. Even dull radiators can be enlivened with metallic paint, turning them from functional but unattractive items into decorative elements. Before using spray paint, completely remove the old paint, then treat the radiator with metal primer. This can then be sprayed over.

NICELY WORN

Gold leaf was traditionally used to decorate furniture, but, unfortunately, it was very easily damaged. As a result, few intact examples survive. However, the distressed look is back in vogue. A similar effect can be achieved by painting a layer of coloured undercoat onto the furniture, followed by a coat of gold paint. This is then rubbed lightly with sandpaper to remove some of the gold and reveal glimpses of the colour beneath.

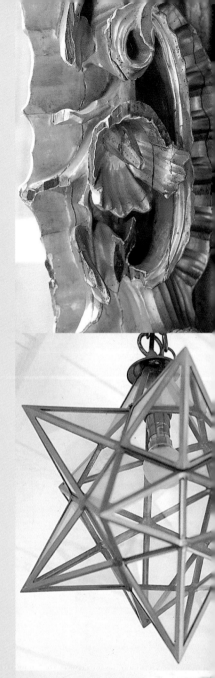

Left
MIRROR FROM THE PAST
With their embellished frames intact, antique mirrors give a real period feel to the home. This 'butler's mirror' was used by staff to keep a discreet eye open for the needs of their master and his guests.

Top right
GLITTERING CURLICUES AND ORNAMENTATION
Furniture can be decorated with gold paint, but gold leaf is still used for picture frames.

Centre right
ILLUMINATED STARS ON THE CEILING
This lamp was found in an antique shop but is actually a replica of a Moorish lantern. Similar lamps can be found in shops selling oriental artefacts.

Bottom right
HEAT SOURCE
This radiator looks warm and inviting thanks to its colour. Painting antique radiators in gold or bronze is an easy way of smartening them up.

Gold brings warmth

It was traditional to decorate picture frames with **gold leaf,** to help give the appearance of a classical interior. In the new classical style, it is more a question of using gold **to provide warmth rather than to convey riches.** For those who want to do the real thing, there are courses in gilding. However, wonders can be performed with **tins and spray cans of gold paint.**

COLOURED UNITS
These simple kitchen units
are made from birch plywood.
Their rich look comes from an
unusual violet-grey stain that is
close to slate in colour. Wood
stains are available in many
colours, in either transparent
or opaque finishes.

The Grand Café style in the kitchen

The ambience of a Parisian café with the clink of glasses and china, relaxing music playing in the background and a tasteful decor can be recreated in your own kitchen. Use materials such as wood, terrazzo and stone, with details in metal for a professional touch. Add **creamy white china** with simple but elegant lines, and **stainless steel kitchen utensils.** The result is neat, classical and stylish.

COLLECTING PORCELAIN

Different shades of creamy white can be a feast for the eyes. Provided you choose designs that are similar, an entire dinner service can be assembled from second-hand china bought from different jumble sales, flea markets and junk shops. The final collection will be unique.

HANDY AND ATTRACTIVE

Where the kitchen units are on view in an open-plan or dining-room/kitchen, they will be more readily incorporated into the design of the room if a strip of material that complements the doors is placed along the edge of the worktop.

Top left
CREAMY PORCELAIN
Simple white china in creamy tones looks good against the warm tones of wood. Most manufacturers of fine china, such as Wedgwood, offer plain white dinner services.

Centre left
ALL EYES ON THE OVEN
An oven as attractive as this deserves to be sited where it can be seen. The cupboard doors are smooth and plain and fill the entire space from floor to worktop, which is flush with the doors, so only the oven front stands out.

Bottom left
TO HAND
A row of small drawers near the hob is handy, and not just for cooking spoons and knives. If they are deep enough, they can hold jars of herbs and spices. Place the name of the herb or spice on the lid and you will easily be able to find what you need.

Right
FUTURE CLASSIC
Heat-resistant glass surrounds this hob. Although the plain plaster wall can still be seen, the glass makes the corner both practical and modern.

Personal style, classically done

FREE-STANDING KITCHEN APPLIANCES
Cooking appliances may be built into units for a streamlined effect but they are also available as free-standing equipment to be placed between the units, as shown on the facing page.

Top left
CLASSICAL WORKING KITCHEN

Modern kitchen equipment is placed among made-to-measure cupboards built in inexpensive materials. There is a welcoming informality about this kitchen and it is clear that the family spends a great deal of time here.

Top right
NUANCES IN GREY

This kitchen proves that grey can be radiantly bright. Extra warmth and interest can be given to terrazzo worktops with the addition of coloured stone, mother-of-pearl or glass.

Bottom left
BEAUTIFUL DOWN TO THE LAST DETAIL

Quality is a feature of classical interiors. In this kitchen, wood, stainless steel and glass have been harmoniously combined.

Bottom right
GENUINE ZINC

Nineteenth-century Parisian bars featured tables and dressers covered in zinc, and these items may still be found in junk and antique shops. If you are really lucky, you might even find an authentic cork remover from the same period. The glasses are thick and robust to evoke a café atmosphere.

Top and bottom left
FOLLOWING OLD EXAMPLES

These classical window catches can be found in older houses, although seldom on every window. Replica replacements are, fortunately, now available.

Centre left
BLACKBOARD

In the black-and-white kitchen, the perfect decoration for the back of the kitchen door or the utility room is blackboard paint. The surface, which can be written on and then wiped clean, is ideal for shopping lists.

Below left
FUN WITH LINES

By placing tiles vertically along the wall instead of horizontally, a border can be created. The black grouting contrasts with the plain white tiles, evoking a sense of the past.

Right
GRAPHIC DETAILS

Old prints and silhouettes are a rich source for many designers, as shown on these curtains. Should you want to design your own, there are copying services that will duplicate images onto fabric for you relatively cheaply.

The basic combination

Black and white will always make a striking combination in the home. **Graphic effects** work particularly well in these colours, which makes designing and living with black and white enormous fun. Sometimes the simplest styles can have the greatest potential.

THOUGHTFUL WITH TILES
The white wall tiling has been broken at waist height with blocks of black for dramatic effect. The mirror above the vanity unit reflects the result on the opposite wall, creating a sense of space. A filing cabinet is a novel idea for storage.

DAMP PROBLEMS WITH MIRRORS
To prevent mirrors being spoiled by damp, either fix them a little away from the wall, so that a small cavity is formed, or fix them into the wall so that no damp can creep behind. For a guaranteed condensation-free reflection, install a heated mirror.

Colour & Contrast

The importance of colour

Colour is the most important element of interior design, and a home decorated around a colour scheme will have a strong and personal style. Colour can create a feeling of space and breathe life into a room. It can affect the way in which light is reflected and so alter the mood of a room. By choosing the colour of unbleached linen or red earth for the walls, bright green and yellow checks for the tablecloth, or perhaps a blue vase for the table, the effect you create will be stunning.

Colour & Contrast

From mood setting to visual surprises

4 CONTENTS

Colour & Contrast

Right

THE PALETTE OF COLOUR AND CONTRAST

Rainbow colours, from sunset yellow to brilliant green, suit bright, contemporary interiors. Although muted shades are not as appropriate to this style of decorating, you could try deeper, more saturated pastel colours, evoking tropical islands with their vibrant flowers, fruit and clear, blue sea.

CHOOSING THE RIGHT COLOUR

Paint colours can be mixed to your individual requirements: in certain stores, scanners will analyse any colour you like – whether from a favourite fabric sample or a magazine photograph – and then work out the correct colour formula for you on computer. Paint colours from the past are also available in heritage ranges, if you are looking for a colour with historical associations.

Colour as inspiration

There are many ways of **living with colour** – in an understated way with subdued colours, or exuberantly with plenty of contrast. Your choice of colour mirrors your personality and determines whether you feel at home in a room. Colour is also a means by which a specific style can be attained or a mood created. All that matters is your **personal preference.**

YELLOW, THE COLOUR OF SUN AND SUMMER

White will probably soon be overtaken by yellow as the most popular colour for walls. Yellow is very versatile: not only is it the colour of the sun, but it can also help to conjure up an oriental atmosphere. Here, a deep, sunset yellow has been combined with a warm red sofa, a table from India and decorative accessories to evoke the mood of the East.

COMBINING COLOURS
By collecting colour
samples in combinations
that you like, you will
get a clear idea of
your favourite colours.
If you want to create
the mood of a
particular country,
it helps to use
association of ideas.
To create the mood
of India, for example,
use the colours of
saris and spices as
a starting point.

COLOUR LINKS
This small room, on a different
level from the adjacent dining-
room, originally had another
entrance. Now the rooms are
linked and also share a colour
scheme. The yellow harmonizes
beautifully with the pine floor,
whilst the fuchsia of the chair
is the main focus of colour.

**WALLPAPER
VERSUS PAINT**
The advantage of
wallpaper is that you
can get an immediate
impression of how it will
look before you hang it.
With paint the effect is
delayed while you wait
for it to dry. It is also
influenced by any
underlying colour and
reflected light. The
advantage of paint is
that it is easier to change
than wallpaper, and a
beautiful result can be
achieved quickly, even
by those who are less
skilled at decorating.

Adapting the available space

SPACIOUS EFFECT
The impression of height in
a room can be influenced by
the choice of colour. Here,
the sloping ceiling above the
door has been painted white,
distinguishing it from the wall,
and making the sloping area
seem less oppressive.

Vibrant colours for furnishing fabrics

**COLOURS FROM
A PAINTER'S PALETTE**
Furnishing fabrics in vibrant
colours, such as lime green,
cobalt and sunflower yellow,
employ every possible motif,
from squares through tie-dye
to flowers or decorative letters.

One space, one colour

Choosing one colour for one space is very **classical.** Traditionally, this was common practice in cottages, and it is now coming back into fashion: a blue room, a red room, and so on. **Colour affects the light,** which is why north-facing rooms are often painted in warm earth colours, whilst blue, sea-green and lilac shades are preferred for rooms facing south.

NATURAL COLOURS
Exploiting the natural tones of metal and wood can be most effective. Wood often has a yellow or brown tinge, whilst that of stainless steel, zinc and aluminium is blue, grey or lilac. The surrounding colours can be finely tuned to match.

Top left

DISPLAY CABINET IN DIFFERENT COLOURS

The front of this wooden display cabinet, found in an antique shop, has been painted reddish-brown. For the back panel, an emerald green was chosen to offset the white porcelain and give the cabinet an impression of greater depth.

Top right

ADVANTAGES OF A DADO

Dado panelling brings various benefits: electricity cables can be hidden away and the lower part of the wall can easily be wiped clean, which is useful if you have small children. Buy ready-to-fix panels from builders' merchants, or design your own using plywood and wooden mouldings.

Bottom left

COOL WITH WARMTH

A staircase and landing can be painted in bold, vibrant colours simply because you spend very little time there and will not be overwhelmed by them. In this example, the strong, warm red compensates for the cool light and enhances the colour of the wood.

Bottom right

TRADITIONAL COLOURS FOR THE BATHROOM

A combination of blue and white is the traditional 'fresh' colour scheme for a bathroom. The mosaic tiles on the wall are made of glass and have a watercolour-like translucence.

Top left
DECORATIONS FOR MORE THAN JUST THE TABLE

A vase of flowers, some earthenware, a candlestick or a dish need not be regarded simply as decorations for the table; they can also be used to great effect on a sideboard or dresser. The slender forms and strong colours used here draw the eye immediately.

Centre left
KEEP IT SIMPLE

Flowers have long been the traditional accompaniment to an elegant dinner service, white, starched napkins and beautifully presented meal. A single bloom laid on a serving dish forms a simple yet stunning centrepiece.

Bottom left
ALTERNATIVE TO TILES

Paint is a viable alternative to wall tiles above the worktop. Painting the plaster in the colour of your choice is cheap as well as quick and simple to change. A final coat of varnish makes the wall waterproof and easier to clean. To avoid scorching, make sure that the hob is not set too close to the wall. An Italian mood has been created in this kitchen with terracotta walls, white units, beech worktops and a classical chequered floor.

Convivial dining

Setting time aside in our busy lives to **dine with family and friends** is becoming increasingly important. Sitting around a table together creates opportunities to renew contacts and strengthen bonds. The dining-room therefore deserves **warm and inviting colours** to evoke a convivial atmosphere that encourages conversation.

**SMALL DETAIL;
BIG IMPACT**
The reddish-orange wall –
actually just two strips of colour
– creates a cosy atmosphere that
is enhanced by the colourful
tableware. The original wooden
cladding of the mansard ceiling
was replaced with replica boards
for an authentic look.

WOOD STAIN in soft watercolour tints can soften the appearance of flooring in south-facing rooms.

LARGE CARPET TILES, when laid diagonally, create the look of an Italian mansion.

LAMINATED FLOORING comes in various timber finishes and a wide range of colours.

GLASS MOSAIC TILES can be laid quickly in blocks of 30 x 30cm (12 x 12in). With the large number of colours available, you can achieve almost any effect you wish.

QUARRY TILES can be bought in their traditional undecorated finish as well as in numerous colours and designs for creating patterns.

CARPETS are available in some outstanding colours. Different-coloured carpets can be cut and laid in pieces to create a striped effect.

Far right

COMBINING various types of floor-covering can create a sense of division between areas. Here traditional floor tiles are used in the hallway, but warm, natural sisal has been laid in the adjoining room. The contrast of vivid and tranquil colours, as well as smooth and hard surfaces, produces unexpected but delightful results.

CLEANING QUARRY TILES
General stains can be mopped up with a liquid abrasive cleaner, while white patches can be treated with a vinegar solution.

Be daring and combine different types of flooring, and let them meet at doorways to **emphasize the contrast.** Sisal that runs into a parquet floor places soft and hard side by side. Let the floor-covering continue part way into the next room for an unusual effect. Make use of the fact that the floor is either the **greatest reflector or absorber of light,** which can influence your choice of colour scheme greatly. Materials and colour are your tools; be sure to use them well.

Contrast in colour and materials on the floor

TILES TO YOUR OWN DESIGN
Specialist tile-makers will produce tiles in your chosen colours and design.

**STAINLESS STEEL
HOB BACK**
Stainless steel is a
good alternative to tiles
for protecting the wall
behind the hob.

Left
**NATURAL HARMONY
OF BEECH WITH YELLOW**
The yellow in the tiles finds
an echo in the warmth of the
beech kitchen units. The tiles
were made to order.

Right
**COLOURFUL KITCHEN,
ITALIAN-STYLE**
Wood and metal seem poles
apart, yet they harmonize
beautifully. The hob and oven
find an echo in the stainless
steel wall-covering, and the
plinths of the orange wooden
cupboards are also finished
with a strip of stainless steel.

Far right
SPACE-SAVER
Practical shelves can be created
in the smallest of spaces. Open
shelves that are narrow yet
deep are an attractive way of
storing crockery and glassware.

Nostalgia with high-tech

A colourful home requires a complementary kitchen. Since the predominant theme is colour, you are therefore completely free to use or combine any decorating styles that take your fancy. The result can be absolutely wonderful, from sober wood with rustic tiles to steel with hot, sunny colours. **In today's kitchen there is room for both high-tech and nostalgia.**

WOODEN FLOORS FOR THE KITCHEN

Smooth cupboard doors are coming back into fashion, often in conjunction with stainless steel. Using a warm material such as wood for the floor prevents a clinical look. Varnished floors soon develop a worn patch near the work surface, and it is difficult to revarnish just a part of the floor; for this reason it is better to impregnate and treat timber floors with wax, which can easily be touched up. The best choices are hardwoods, but avoid oak because water will stain it.

New uses
for tried
and tested
materials

Top left
CURVES IN THE KITCHEN
Beech is the perfect material for kitchen worktops because it is hygienic and fairly water-resistant. Rounded-off edges and corners are far more attractive than right angles, and can be machined to order.

Top right
MEDITERRANEAN TIME
The owner of this kitchen took her inspiration from the Mediterranean. The simple beauty of the white tiles has a clean, contemporary appeal, and a note of variation was added with a border of tiles laid vertically. The minimalist clock fits the scheme of things.

Bottom left
CLEVERLY USED
To add textural interest to the ceiling, the previously white beams were roughly sanded to allow the colour of the wood to show through. Given that there is rarely enough storage space in a kitchen, it is a good idea to put any unused space to work – including that above your head. You will never again have to hunt for a pan deep in the back of a cupboard.

Bottom right
DRAWERS ON WHEELS
New ideas are entering the kitchen. This transparent plastic trolley, with its stainless steel frame and four deep drawers, is easy to use as well as a pleasure to look at.

WHITE AS A FEATURE
White plaster mouldings make excellent contrasting borders in areas of solid colour.

SIMPLY RED
This staircase, seen earlier in the book, has been kept simple but dramatic by painting it in one vibrant colour. The unusual balusters are white to stop them competing with the red.

RADIATOR GRILLE
The grille covering this radiator is made of metal, but similar grilles can also be found in wood. For replacement antique radiator knobs, search in an architectural salvage yard.

FULLY COORDINATED
Silver, glass, chrome, white and blue all have a fresh and clean look, making them the ideal choice for bathrooms.

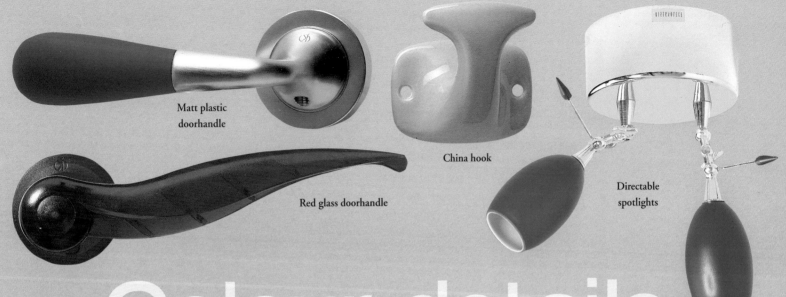

Matt plastic
doorhandle

China hook

Directable
spotlights

Red glass doorhandle

Colour details

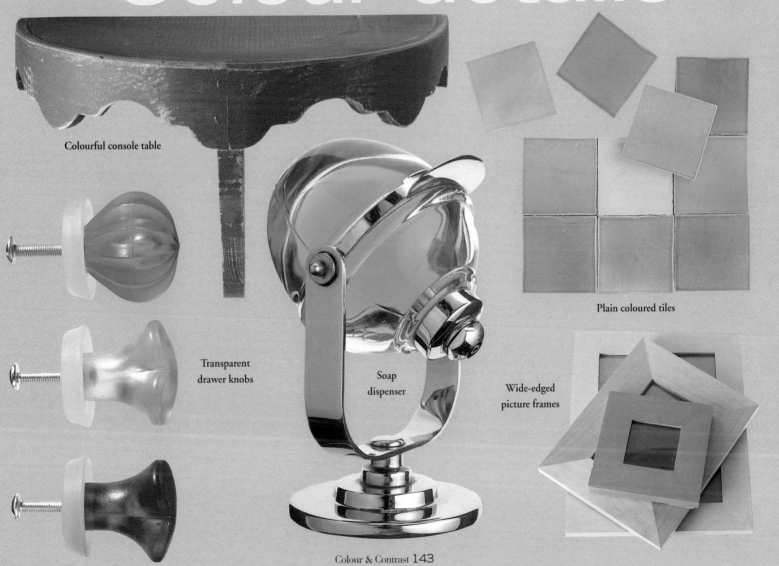

Colourful console table

Transparent
drawer knobs

Soap
dispenser

Plain coloured tiles

Wide-edged
picture frames

CLASSICAL MOTIF
The sun motif has a classical style that gives this bright and airy room a timeless charm.

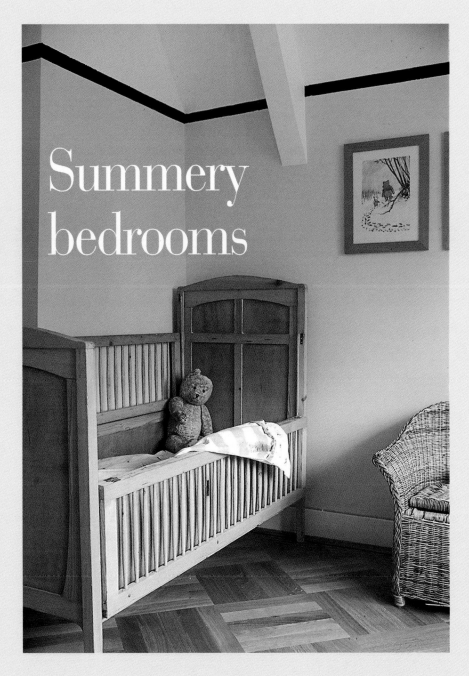

Summery bedrooms

Left
NOSTALGIC WALL

A border of paint or wallpaper at picture-rail height helps to create a more intimate feeling in a room with a high ceiling.

Right
DISGUISED DOOR

A doorway that is no longer used can be hidden behind a cupboard; alternatively it can be used as a frame for a new cupboard. This mobile shelf unit was built to the precise measurements of the doorway. Baskets on the shelves in place of drawers are useful for carrying in clothes for ironing.

More fabric is generally used in the bedroom than anywhere else in the home. This offers plenty of opportunity for creating **fantastic effects** with bold designs, especially as a bed cover can quite easily, and relatively cheaply, be replaced. It is a good idea to **paint the walls** in just one colour, choosing a shade that stands out. Consider **fresh lime green,** for example.

Top left
BED LINEN IN RESERVE
Bed linen that complements your bedroom colour scheme provides the perfect finishing touch. You might consider buying rather more than you need just in case the design is discontinued by the time the linen needs replacing.

Centre left
BRIGHT COLOURS
Lightweight blankets in bright colours are perfect for late summer when it is too hot for a duvet but too cool for sheets.

Bottom left
SQUARES, FLOWERS AND STRIPES
Lots of pillows and generous bed covers in squares, stripes and brightly coloured flowers make a bedroom inviting.

Right
TROPICAL NIGHTS
The mosquito net brings to mind distant lands. As well as being useful on hot summer nights, it also lends a romantic air to the bedroom. During the day it can be twisted into a rope and lightly tied into a loop. It can then be let down at night in one easy movement.

Bed linen with a new look

IDEAS FOR COLOUR
The combination of white with multicoloured floral designs creates a summery bedroom all year round. The old-fashioned bedstead adds a rustic touch.

YESTERDAY'S BED, TODAY'S COMFORT
Old-style iron bedsteads, complete with good quality bases, are enjoying a revival.

Top left
BE DARING
Bold elements, such as the humorous painting and extra large floor tiles, enliven this hallway. The second-hand sideboard has been painted a strong green to contrast with the wall and chequered floor.

Top right
PRETTY PICTURE
Still-lifes occur spontaneously in the home, inspiring colour combinations that you might never have considered.

Bottom left
FLORAL INSPIRATION
Flowers have been a source of inspiration for artists through the ages and for all who love colour in their home. Flowers often have intense colours that vary in tone from petal to petal. This effect can be copied with emulsion paint and fabrics.

Right
CONTRASTING DESIGN
Although the pattern of this throw is in complete contrast to that of the sofa, a delightful colour balance is created.

If you choose strong colours, it is advisable to keep the furniture **classic, timeless and simple,** so that the colours themselves can play the leading role.

Accessories are ideal for trying out **new thoughts and ideas** because you can experiment with them until the desired effect is achieved.

Classic shapes
in colour

Walls that come alive

THE STYLE OF AN OLD HOUSE

The look of an old house can sometimes be recreated with colourwashes – a technique widely used in new houses to give a feeling of age. The walls can be made less smooth by adding special finishes.

Top left

THE COTTAGE LOOK

Adding texture to a wall is easy with a colourwash; a few layers of paint will produce an ageing effect. The door has also been treated with a colourwash.

Top right

SPONGING, DRAGGING AND DABBING

The character and texture of a surface can be influenced by the use of sponges, cloths or wide brushes. The way in which the paint is applied also has an effect, whether you use circles, broad sweeps or light dabs. A radiator and pipes painted the same colour as the wall will appear less obtrusive.

Bottom left and right

COLOURWASH AS BACKGROUND

The relaxed and informal look of a colourwash lends itself to small bedrooms and convivial corners with collections of photographs, postcards or prints. Tints such as yellow or orange create an Italian feel.

Right

DUTCH INSPIRATION

The inspiration for this room, with its red-and-white check armchair against a wall covered with ultramarine colourwash paper, comes from traditional Dutch interiors.

Far right

AN IDEAL CONTRAST

Soft orange colourwashed walls are the perfect contrast to the wooden basin surround.

COLOURWASH: BOOKS THAT TELL YOU HOW
Colourwashing is fun to do, but if you have never tried it before, there are many books about special painting and decorating techniques that will give you all the guidance you need.

Colourwash means, quite simply, washing with colours. **Walls come to life** with this technique and rooms get a **lived-in, rustic character.** Colourwashing starts with a light undercoat to which the colour is applied with a wide distemper brush. The paint is then either rubbed in circles with a wet flannel wrapped in cloth, or dabbed with a sponge. For a **powdery effect** you can apply diluted white paint over a coat of colour. Special colourwash paints are available from shops, but ordinary emulsion works perfectly well. **Bold experimentation produces the best results.**

Moving away from classic white

Glass mosaic tiles are available in many styles and colours. Their translucent properties give the bathroom a cool, aquatic feel. Waterproofing bathroom walls is an alternative to tiling, as it opens up more possibilities for decoration. **Wooden panelling** can also look very attractive in a bathroom.

Left

**MAKING THE MOST OF
EXISTING FEATURES**

Making use of existing features
can deliver very pleasing results.
The original, glass-fronted
cupboard was kept during the
redecoration of this bathroom,
and in the new layout, there is
space beneath it for the bath.

Right

TRADITIONAL DETAILS

This unusual vanity unit has
been made by cutting out the
top of an old table to take a
basin. The finishing touch is
the traditional-style mixer tap.
The wood has been protected
with waterproofing paint.

**ANTIQUE-STYLE
BATHROOM FITTINGS**
Reproduction
sanitary ware, taps
and fittings are widely
available, providing the
finishing touches to
a classical bathroom.

Top left
SIMPLE FEATURES SET THE STYLE
Style can be created without grand gestures. A single, old-fashioned tap set in the wall above a marble basin with a chrome wastepipe are the small details that suggest both refinement and grandeur.

Centre left
CLASSIC FEATURES
Antique objects can dictate a look. To display this French mirror, the mosaic stops part way up the wall, and the remaining plaster is decorated in a dreamy shade of lavender.

Bottom left
BEHIND FALSE WALLS
False walls can make bathroom improvements easier as pipes can be hidden away behind them. If the walls stop at half the height of the bathroom, they provide handy shelving for lotions and potions.

Mediterranean
summer hues

Far left
**LOVE AFFAIR WITH
WARMER CLIMES**

Holidays in warmer climates
give you the opportunity to see
what can be achieved with tile
designs. They can be delightful
in the home, especially in the
bathroom. The pattern on this
floor is repeated on the wall.

Left
THINKING BIG

A washbasin surround can
be made from a wide range
of materials, including wood,
stone and terrazzo. This top
is made of concrete, with black
toner added to the mix. On
another base it would seem far
too big, but the generous size
of the basin, the strong cobalt
blue of the tiles, combined
with the sturdy supports, make
for an unusual, stylish result.

Practicalities

Renovation to repairs

5

CONTENTS

Planning and preparation

Many look back on their first efforts at do-it-yourself and declare: 'The next time I'm going to do all this properly.' The things you ought to know before you start usually come to light only when you have encountered the problems. For example, what to do with all those leads from the television, telephone and lamps that are running across the living-room floor? How to cope with blistering in the newly painted ceiling? Why won't the new fireplace draw the smoke properly?

The final chapter of this book therefore provides basic information on practical matters related to making a home, and tips on how to deal with possible problems. It is intended not as a complete do-it-yourself guide (although it does include a mini-course in painting and decorating) but more as a support for an important stage in your home-making: the planning and preparation before the work gets underway.

Buying a home

Buying a home is one of the most exciting times in life, but making the right decision requires some careful thinking as well as enthusiasm. Choosing the right property for you depends on understanding your living requirements and your aspirations. Home purchase often coincides with other significant changes in life, such as a marriage or a new relationship, or the arrival of a baby or other addition to the household. These changes may impose previously unanticipated demands on the home, which need to be taken into consideration. Buying a house is considered to be an extremely stressful undertaking, with anxieties over poor surveys, breaks in the chain of purchasers/vendors, and timetabling the move itself to contend with. Try to remain calm: the result will be worth it.

DECIDING WHAT YOU NEED

Start by asking yourself some basic questions to help you form an idea of what you are really looking for: How many bedrooms and reception rooms do you want? Is a garden important to you or will it be a burden to maintain? Do you want to live in a city, town or village environment? Will access via stairs be a problem or do you need a property on one level? Do you want a single- or multi-storey property? Do you want to buy a new property or an older but well-maintained one? Do you want to design your own living space, and would therefore find rebuilding, remodelling, converting or building anew a more flexible and cost-effective option? Will the upheaval of any building work be an inconvenience to you or to any other member of the household?

DOMESTIC BUDGET

A good place to start is to work out how much you can afford to pay. For this purpose it is sensible to work out your domestic budget. To do this, you should set out your income and expenditure in two columns next to each other. Income includes salary, bonuses and other fixed payments to you. On the opposite side there are three types of expenditure: the fixed costs (including insurances, local rates, energy costs and the telephone) which are payable at set intervals; household costs, for example food, clothing, running repairs to house and garden, and entertainment; and third, major expenditure for things like furniture or foreign holidays. A quick way to get an overview of these costs is to look at your bank statements for the previous year. Most lenders will help you to assess your domestic budget, often with the aid of a domestic budget calculator or estimator.

MORTGAGES

Once you have an idea of your living costs, you can start the process of looking for a mortgage. Banks, mortgage brokers, estate agents and other lenders can provide you with more information. With their advice, and by asking extensive questions about the current interest rate, repayments, and terms and conditions, you can decide which is the most suitable mortgage for you. If your new home is likely to need improvements or repairs, ask whether these costs can be included in your mortgage. Home loans are available to help buy properties in need of rebuilding, converting or for buying land and building anew.

It is a good idea to leave yourself some financial breathing space. If you borrow the maximum permissible amount you could find yourself unable to pay for work that you had not anticipated but which, nevertheless, is essential. You will also be vulnerable to any rises in mortgage repayment rates.

A READY-MADE HOME

If you do not want to get involved in anything other than furnishing or decorating your home, then you are likely to want to find a property that is either new, or in very good structural condition. The price is likely to reflect the fact that very little or no work is required – new properties may even carry a price premium.

REBUILDING

If you intend to have a greater influence on the interior design and room arrangement of your home, then you will probably find it more cost-effective to buy a property already requiring structural repairs, as the price will reflect the amount of work that needs to be done. Properties in need of modernization, repair or renovation are a good option if you do not want to take on too much work

> **FINANCE FIRST**
> Before you rush out to buy the home of your dreams, think very carefully about the financial implications. Affordability is a big factor in choosing the right home.

and too big a mortgage, but want to stamp your identity on your home. This can still be a good way to get more home for your money, especially if you are prepared to get involved in some of the work yourself on a DIY basis. Common requirements are the installation of new plumbing and wiring, new sanitaryware and kitchen units, and repairs to the basic structure. It is usually relatively easy to move internal partition walls, if you want to re-arrange the room layout, or to remove them altogether. Sections of floor on an upper level may even be removed if you want to create double height areas, and staircases too can be moved.

Look out for properties that still have many of their period features intact, like original doors and windows, flooring, mouldings and fireplaces. These can be restored or stripped and refinished and can make wonderful features. Do not be put off by the condition of existing decoration or furnishing, or the state of the garden, all of which can easily be changed. Look out for properties that offer the potential for extension or attic conversion. This extra accommodation can add value to your home, but check with the local authorities about any building restrictions before buying.

CONVERSION

Some of the most unusual homes have been built in structures that were formerly used for some other purpose. The ever increasing change from agrarian to industrial-based economies in the developed nations has left redundant a huge range of former agricultural buildings, such as old barns and mills, often in idyllic rural locations.

POTENTIAL FOR CONVERSION

In many countries, some churches and other places of worship are vacant and falling into disrepair. Although sometimes difficult to convert, especially if set in consecrated ground, the results can be spectacular.

Other buildings that may offer potential space in which to create your home include old schools, offices, hospitals, watermills and windmills, lighthouses and even prisons. Amongst the more unusual choices for conversion have been an old air raid shelter, the arches of an old railway bridge, a cricket pavilion, several underground reservoirs and an air traffic control tower.

These can frequently be bought extremely cheaply, although converting them into homes or apartments that meet today's exacting building regulations can be fairly expensive. Concurrent with this migration from the countryside to the towns, there has also been a decline in large-scale industry and a tendency to relocate businesses from expensive city offices to much cheaper out-of-town sites. This has left a number of warehouses, factories and other former industrial buildings redundant. Some are sufficiently small to form a single dwelling, but most are large buildings that are spilt up into individual units by property developers and then bought by private individuals. Sold as a shell, such buildings can present an exciting opportunity to design a home from scratch within an existing structure, in an otherwise completely built-up area, often in the centre of a town or city. Such spaces can often be light and airy, lending themselves to some very innovative modern designs. On the downside, they can be difficult and expensive to heat, due to their size.

Before purchasing any property for conversion into a home, it is essential to get a clear idea of the costs that will be involved by commissioning a survey and consulting a building professional, such as an architect, building surveyor or structural engineer. They will be able to assess the suitability of the structure for your intended use and will also be able to help assess the cost of bringing water, electricity, telephone and other essential services to the property.

BUILDING YOUR OWN HOME

Where building land is available, designing and building a new house from scratch offers the greatest freedom to create your own personally designed living environment. Providing you comply with the local design and building regulations, which you should check before buying a site, you can create whatever sort of home you want, modern or traditional, with a room plan arranged exactly as you want. This can be a very cost-effective way of creating an individual home, as building a new property is often less expensive per square metre of living space than converting or rebuilding an existing structure. For further advice, consult a professional designer such as an architect or surveyor.

LOCATION

Location is one of the most important factors to consider when buying or building a home. As well as thinking about where you would like to live, think of the practicalities such as proximity to friends and family, work, shops and schools. Travelling may not be a problem today, but commuting is becoming increasingly time-consuming and expensive as the number of cars per capita increases.

CHECKING THE PROPERTY

Before purchasing any property, make sure that you arrange for an appropriately qualified expert to undertake a survey to assess the suitability of the property for your intended use. Even new buildings may have faults, and it pays to be aware of what these are before parting with your money.

If you are planning rebuilding or conversion work, a detailed survey is absolutely vital. The professional inspector, usually a surveyor, will prepare a report that will detail the structural condition of the property, and any repairs that are required, possibly with an indication of the likely cost of reinstatement

SYMPATHETIC RENOVATION
Whether extending, renovating or converting, it is important to build in sympathy with the existing structure, both in terms of architectural style and choice of materials. This is also true for new properties built in areas that have a strong visual identity which could be compromised by an inappropriate new development

work. The surveyor's report can also be used to gain estimates from builders for the work. Any information discovered during the survey inspection can be used to renegotiate the purchase price with the vendor. Before appointing any professional, make sure you take references and check that they are appropriately insured and a member of the relevant trade association or body. Agree the price and details in writing of any work you want them to under-take before the work commences, and ensure that each of you keeps a signed copy.

CAREFUL BUDGETING

If you are planning extensive renovation or conversion work, or are building your own home, prepare your budget carefully by talking to builders and professionals. Allow for alternative accommodation whilst work is underway, professionals' fees, connection of services such as water, gas and electricity and a 10 per cent contingency sum.

Planning
the interior

Everything seems possible in a new property or one that is being extensively renovated or remodelled. It is great fun visiting DIY, fabric and furniture shops and deciding how to furnish and decorate. Although it may be easier to decide on some of these things after you have lived in your home for a while, it is sensible to work out from the outset what style of furniture will fit and what sizes the various pieces can be.

Do you yearn to buy new furniture even before the construction work is finished, or have you not yet decided how to furnish your new home? To help you with the dimensions and proportions of the rooms and possible furnishings, it is a good idea to make a plan of the floor area. It will help greatly with deciding how to use the space in the home. A scale of 1:20 gives a good impression (1cm = 20cm in reality, or 1in = 20in in reality). Try using squared paper – the grid makes drawing any plans much easier.

REMOVING WALLS

Once you have a plan, it is easy to try out lots of different ideas, moving or removing the walls or adding extra space until you reach a room layout that suits your lifestyle and aspirations. In reality, a builder or architect will advise you whether it is safe to remove a particular wall or whether openings

can be created. New walls can easily be constructed from plasterboard and timber studwork or with lightweight concrete blocks. Archways can be created using special metal forms which can be plastered over.

ARRANGING THE FURNITURE

Use a similar 1:20 plan for arranging the furniture. Draw each piece of furniture as seen from above to the same scale and cut out the drawings. Now you can move the paper furniture around as often as you need to see how your real furniture will fit in the new home. Try to visualize the end result and bear in mind the space needed to walk around the room and between furniture. Do not forget to allow for the space that is needed to open doors and windows (if these open inwards) and allow enough room to pass by without bumping into them.

DIVIDING WITH FURNITURE

Rooms can be divided with furniture as well as with walls. A sideboard or dresser, a dining table or free-standing storage units can all be used to section off parts of a room (see illustration top far right). A more spacious effect is achieved if the cupboard does not reach higher than 50cm (20in) from the ceiling, so that the ceiling is seen to continue. This is particularly important in smaller living areas. The right height for cupboards against the walls needs to be related to the distance between them and the rest of the furniture and also to the width of the room. A tall bookcase less than 3m (10ft) in front of a sofa can seem intimidating. In such a case it is better to place the bookcase to the side or behind the field of view and to have a lower cupboard in front of you.

DETERMINING SPACE: THE FLOOR TO CEILING HEIGHT

The floor and ceiling play an important role in the spatial arrangement of the home. The finish and colour of the flooring and walls have an influence, but more important are their heights and levels. To create a more intimate area with a large room, an area of raised or sunken floor or a change in ceiling levels can be used as a division, without losing the sense of spaciousness.

DESIGNING IN 3-D

Many interior designers prefer to work in three dimensions rather than on a flat piece of paper. The simplest way to do this is to make a small-scale model of the living space and furniture items from cardboard. This is considerably easier than it sounds – rather like making a small dolls' house – and can reveal many problems that are not immediately apparent when working in only two dimensions. An even easier way of visualizing your ideas in 3-D is with the help of a home or interior design programme on a personal computer. Most households now have access to a personal computer, and home and interior design software packages are inexpensive and simple to use.

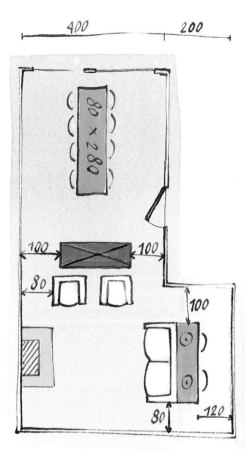

Left
A small wall set at an angle to one of the main walls can form a discrete study area, as well as providing some useful extra shelving.

Right
A cupboard between two parts of a room creates two separate areas – one for dining and the other for relaxing – and provides more storage space.

Annotated measurements are in centimetres: 90cm = 3ft

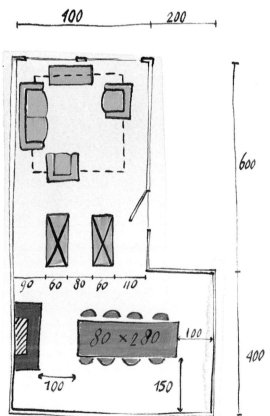

Left
Partitions that do not reach to the ceiling make a room feel more spacious. Here a dressing area has been provided behind the bed.

Right
For more light in the room, two cupboards can be arranged in parallel formation, as in a library. The necessary circulation space within and between the two separate areas is maintained.

Installations

Installations in the home include the central heating and ventilation, electrical wiring, and plumbing. The installation of any of these has to comply with the legal safety regulations of your local area. These regulations may seem to be an obstacle to some of your more creative ideas, but they contribute greatly to safety in the home.

Turn the water off and undo the nut.

Connect the valve to the radiator and pipe.

Fix the knob on the valve and adjust it.

PLANNING AHEAD
During rebuilding or adding an extension it is a good idea to put trunking or ducting in the wall. This can be used later for loudspeaker or other cables for video and audio equipment.

HOT WATER SYSTEM

Central heating systems that are separate from the hot water system are increasingly being replaced by combination boilers that fire the central heating and provide hot water on demand. These are particularly appropriate for smaller properties, where the demand on heating and hot water is light. Larger households with two or more bathrooms may prefer some form of hot water storage, especially if baths are used, as demand may outstrip the boiler's ability to heat water. This may be a small 'side saddle' cylinder, added to a combination boiler, or a separate boiler and hot water cylinder.

The energy efficiency of your boiler will have a huge influence on your running costs, so consider investing in a condensing or other type of high efficiency model.

Where the local water pressure is sufficient, a mains pressure plumbing system may be appropriate, providing excellent flow rates without the need for a cold water storage or header tank in the attic. Such systems also eliminate the requirement for pumps on showers, as the pressure is already sufficient for a satisfyingly exhilarating flow.

Installing a hot water system yourself is possible, but make sure you know about the correct connection of the flow and return pipes, the distance apart they must be, and the connection of thermostatic valves (see left). These all have a major part to play in the efficiency of the system.

THE MOST POWERFUL SHOWER JET

The pressure of the shower jet will depend on two factors: the type of equipment installed and the flow rates and temperatures of the hot and cold water supply. Mixer showers are available with manual temperature controls, which may need to be adjusted if the flow rate of hot or cold water varies because of demand elsewhere in the home. Showers with built-in thermostatic flow controls are also available; these will adjust their own flow rate to maintain a constant, preselected temperature, regardless of changes in pressure.

The hot water flow rate will depend on the type of boiler and tank installed and the cold water flow rate that supplies it. If the pressure is inadequate for any reason, a pumped or power shower system should be installed.

BATH AND SHOWER USED TOGETHER

A shower uses about 8–15 litres (1³/₄–3 ¹/₄ gal) of hot water per minute and the average bath about 15–30 litres (3¹/₄–6¹/₂ gal). A cylinder with a capacity of 80 litres (17¹/₂ gal) per minute is therefore necessary if both are to be used at once.

CHOOSING YOUR HEATING FUEL

Choosing which fuel to use to heat your home will depend on local availability, installation and running costs, convenience, and any evnironmental concerns that you may have.

THE ELECTRICAL WIRING

Should you decide to wire or rewire your home, remember that safety is of paramount importance. Each area has its own safety regulations and it is important first to find out what these are and then to comply with them. Before the electrical circuit can be connected to the supply on new properties, it will have to be officially checked by the local electricity company. For rebuilding or remodelling projects, ensure that the supply is switched off before starting any work. Electricity is particularly dangerous in rooms that become wet, i.e. kitchens and bathrooms, and so the rules on installation in these areas are very strict. It is possible to undertake wiring and rewiring on a DIY basis, and a diagram drawn to scale is very useful in creating a wiring plan. You can draw in all the switches and sockets you need in each room, plan your circuits and calculate how much wire is needed. If you want feature lighting, perhaps with different circuits for table, wall and ceiling lights, then plan it now.

SPECIAL COMPUTER CONNECTIONS

It is advisable to have a dedicated circuit for the power supply to a computer. This prevents interference from other equipment sharing the circuit. It is also worth installing a device that will protect the computer from fluctuations in the current which could damage the equipment.

SEPARATE CIRCUITS
The following equipment is best connected to its own circuit: washing machine and dryer ● cooker ● immersion heater ● dishwasher ● outdoor circuits ● computer

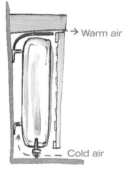

→ Warm air

Cold air

Make sure that there is an adequate through flow of air when boxing in a radiator.

VENTILATION

Good ventilation is essential to prevent the build-up of condensation and moisture which may damage the fabric of the building. Ventilation should remove damp, stale air, and replace it with dry, fresh air from outside the building, thus creating a balance of air flow. Ventilation is particularly important in wet areas, such as the kitchen and bathrooms, and most areas now have strict rules to ensure that properties are adequately ventilated. Ventilation can also be used to extract smells and some allergens.

TYPES OF VENTILATION SYSTEM

There are ducted and surface-mounted ventilation systems. The first type can be installed in tubular ducts, but this out-of-sight variety can usually only be installed during the early stages of building. Ventilation is provided by one of two methods: mechanical fans or using the principle of convection.

Wall-mounted ventilation systems are usually in the form of an extractor fan that can be connected to a light switch. Some models even continue working for a given length of time after the light has been switched off. These are highly suitable for toilets There are also models with a humidity detector. These switch off only when the humidity has been reduced sufficiently.

Original details

Those who chose an older house have chosen the charm and architecture of the past. Sometimes, however, such a house has been modernized and all the original features have been removed or hidden behind panelling. There are countless specialist suppliers of old building materials that can help you bring your home back to its original look. Alternatively, you can contact architectural salvage suppliers and try to find originals.

LEADED GLASS

If the leaded glass is missing, there are two ways to discover what used to be there. There may be houses in the vicinity that still have their leaded glass intact. Ask the owners if you may take photographs of it. Then you can ask a specialist in leaded glass to copy the design for you. If there are no examples to be found, a specialist leaded glass studio can advise you on the style best suited to your home. If you have a steady hand and are feeling ambitious, sign up for a course in leaded glass and make your own window. It is somewhat different when the window needs to provide insulation or security. You can opt for new double glazing with leaded glass inserted between the panes. The studio will have contacts for this process. Another possibility is to install secondary glazing.

REMOVING OLD PAINT FINISHES

Panel doors or banisters with attractive spindles are often covered in layers of dirty old paint and/or varnish. You can clean them yourself, but if you use a scraper there is a strong possibility that you will damage fine moulding and detail, whilst sandpapering intricate designs can be very tiresome and not always satisfactory. Specialist companies can remove all the layers of old paint, varnish and grime using lye (a strong alkaline solution) without damaging the details or harming the glue in the joints. Bear in mind that they cannot work at your home, so you will need to dismantle everything to take it to them. Windows can also be treated, although the glazing will have to be removed if it is held in place by putty rather than glazing beads, as the putty may be

removed with the paint. The process is not cheap, and items may still require some cleaning afterwards. Before making a decision, make sure that the item is worth stripping.

MAKING A REPLICA

Sometimes an ornamental feature indoors or out is damaged or has bits missing, or one of a pair has vanished completely. Think of banister spindles, for instance, or decorative features on the exterior wall, or perhaps ornamental brackets supporting a beam or the ceiling. It may be possible to find an old replacement from a salvage yard, but in most cases it will be easier to find a new replacement. A wide range of replicas of period items are available from many suppliers, and these are likely to be a more cost-effective option than going for an original. If, however, your missing feature is very unusual, then you may need to have a replacement made especially, and there are companies that specialize in this area of work. Timber items are usually simple to replicate, and if a wooden finish is intended, it may even be possible to find a piece of old timber that matches the original. Alternatively, wood can be aged and coloured. Contact a specialist carpenter, wood turner or wood carver. Stone masons will also be able to carve replacement items, although for

complicated shapes in stone it is often cheaper to make a mould from the original and then to cast a replacement using a mixture of stonedust and white cement, mixed to reach a colour match.

RESTORING OLD FLOORS

Beneath the floor-covering of rooms or halls in older properties there is often a lovely wooden, tiled or stone floor that only needs to be cleaned and finished to look like new.

Wooden floors and stairs will usually require some sanding before they can be refinished. Mechanical sanders are available for hire in most towns and will take the work out of cleaning a large area; small hand-held electric models can be used for smaller or inaccessible areas. Remember to remove any protruding nails or other obstacles that may damage the sander before starting work, and make sure that the area is well ventilated. Although very efficient, mechanical sanders do produce an enormous amount of dust, so it is sensible to cover or remove furniture, and to put heavy tape around any

internal doors in order to prevent dust spreading all over the house. If you find the dust unpleasant, it might be wise to wear a mask; these are available from pharmacists. Start with a coarse grade sandpaper to remove major marks and gradually work down to a fine grade.

A wide variety of finishes are available for wooden floors, ranging from simple natural oils and waxes through to hard-wearing polyurethane polishes. There are also a number of products available for colouring wood, either as separate dyes or as ready-coloured oils, waxes and finishes. Wooden parquet floors can be treated in the same way as wooden boards. However, if the blocks have lifted or sunk, it may be necessary to remove them and then to relay a level substrate onto which the blocks can be positioned.

Stone flooring should not be sanded and may require a chemical cleaning agent. Specialist advice should be sought, as stone is easily damaged and discoloured when exposed, and can be very costly to replace.

Insulation

New homes are usually built with energy conservation in mind and so are well insulated. With alterations to older properties, this should be one of the first areas to attend to; the results should be improved comfort and lower heating bills. Improving insulation is also often part of major repairs.

EXCESSIVE INSULATION

Insulation is of benefit only if it is properly carried out. If not, it may even cause damage. Insulation does not mean closing off every chink and seam. Cooking and bathing put water vapour into the air and if it cannot escape, it will condense on the nearest part of the house that is cold. This is usually the window frames, glass of the windows, and the ground floor, which can be damaged by excessive damp. Good ventilation is the principal remedy for condensation. This can be achieved by, for instance, having ventilation grills built into the window frames. Daily airing is essential for a home. Dry air can be heated more quickly than damp air.

THE BEST INSULATION

The following points are worth noting:
- Ensure that there is a small air cavity between the existing wall and the layer of insulation.
- Fix a damp-proof membrane between the insulation and the finishing layer of the wall (often plasterboard that is finished with plaster). For a partition wall made of either metal or timber studs, the insulation layer is fixed between the uprights. A damp-proof layer is then fixed to the framework, followed by the plasterboard and its coat of plaster.

If there is a cavity wall, the house can be insulated by filling the cavity with a special insulation medium. Older houses rarely have cavity walls.

INSULATING FLOORS

A significant amount of heat is lost through the floor of a building, yet this is an area that people often forget to insulate. If the floor is of suspended construction, then there will be a void beneath the floor into which insulation can be installed. Where the flooring is laid directly on to a substrate, then a space for the insulation must be created below the floor. This can be done by removing and relaying the substrate, so as not to raise the finished floor level, which can prevent doors from opening. If raising the floor level is not a problem, then the flooring material can be removed and relaid onto battens, which lift the floor to create a space for the insulation.

INSULATING WITH GLASS

Double or even triple glazing can help save a considerable amount of energy. The insulation value of the different types varies. There are situations where double glazing cannot be used: there may be too little depth to the window frames, or perhaps attractive antique leaded lights. In these cases secondary glazing can be used, installed on either the inside or outside of the property. Do not replace original windows simply in order to have double glazing, as you are likely to damage the character of the property. If you feel that double glazing is not suitable, then try adding extra insulation elsewhere, such as in the roof or under the floor, and fit a more efficient heating system. Before doing any of these, seal all the draughts.

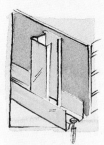

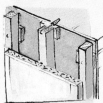

Outside wall insulation seen from indoors, on wooden or steel frames.

> Glass with a high level of insulation is available; it is coated with a layer that prevents radiant heat from escaping. The void between the glazing units can also be filled with an inert gas, such as argon, which further limits the conduction of heat through the unit.

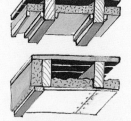

Four methods to insulate floors, depending upon the space beneath.

> ### DAMP-REDUCING LAYER
> It is important to place a layer that reduces damp on the warm side (indoors) to prevent the insulation material becoming wet, which would remove its insulating properties. Before treating the problem of damp, try and treat the cause, which is usually poor ventilation.

METHODS OF INSULATING A ROOF

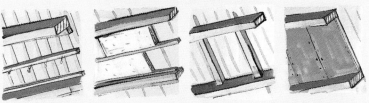

Retain character by placing insulation between the rafters, then covering it.

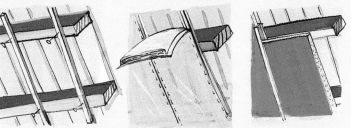

If you want the timber to be hidden, fix insulation panels to the rafters.

Poorly fitting windows and doors can cause horrible draughts that can make even a well-heated home uncomfortable. One option is to replace or repair the windows and doors or their frames, though it is usually possible to alleviate the problem by installing a draughtstrip. Several types are available, usually with a self-adhesive strip on one side and either a brush or other flexible material on the other. These can often be fitted on a DIY basis to the inside of the frame, and if there is sufficient space in the frame runner, these will be quite unobtrusive. You may need to call in a professional if hinges have to be moved.

Major repairs

During a structural survey, all the areas of a property that deteriorate and that are easily accessed will be carefully examined by a professional surveyor. Such a survey is essential before buying any property, particularly if it is for rebuilding, remodelling or conversion to residential use. The findings will allow the suitability of the building for its intended use to be assessed, along with the likely costs of building or repair work. This information can be used to negotiate a fair purchase price.

THE STRUCTURAL SURVEY

During a structural house survey, each of the floors is assessed on many points – the skirting-boards, ridge tiles, window frames, hinges and locks, central heating, insulation and ventilation. The report indicates the condition of all these parts of the property, whether repairs are needed immediately and what the eventual costs are likely to be.

GRANTS AND TAX CONCESSIONS

Local or national government may offer grants, tax concessions or other financial assistance for properties that are being rebuilt, remodelled or converted. Contact local or regional building authorities for details of relevant schemes.

WOODWORM

During the structural survey, the timber in the property should be checked for woodworm. Holes in wood and wood dust on the floor are an indication of the presence of these larvae. Wood wasps, fungi and lichen can also cause problems. If the structure has not been so badly damaged that replacement is needed, a specialist company can deal with the problem. Only have this work carried out after the timber in the house has been checked. If the problem is wet or dry rot or some other fungal infection, then your problem is likely to be poor ventilation. Solve this problem first (see pages 162–3 for ideas) and then replace only those timbers that are structurally damaged.

DAMP IN THE HOME

Penetrating damp is almost always due to bad pointing or rendering of the external walls. In such a case the joints in the masonry have to be raked out and repointed after the walls have been cleaned. The rendering must be repaired or replaced. These measures are usually sufficient to solve the damp problem. Rising damp damages the floor joists and other timber constructions, and efficient under-floor ventilation is essential to protect them.

Damp can also damage the plaster on the inside walls. In this event, the walls will need to be impregnated to just beneath the floor joists to prevent the damp from rising up the walls. It can also help if the metal flashing is replaced, particularly if a wall adjoins a balcony that does not drain well.

EXTERNAL TIMBER ROT

Neglected maintenance to guttering and painting and also inadequate under-floor ventilation can result in rotten timber. To prevent this, the roofing and flashing must be replaced when they show signs of deterioration. The areas most prone to rot are those that suffer the greatest exposure to the elements, such as the soffits (under the eaves or roof overhang) and the fascia boards (the boards to which the rainwater system is attached). Regular maintenance and painting will restrict damage to these areas.

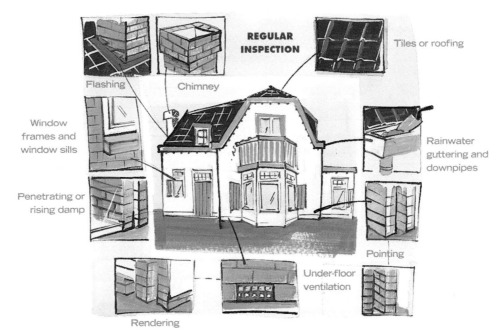

REGULAR INSPECTION

Flashing

Chimney

Tiles or roofing

Window frames and window sills

Penetrating or rising damp

Rainwater guttering and downpipes

Pointing

Under-floor ventilation

Rendering

REPAIRING WINDOW FRAMES

Rotten window frames can be repaired if the damage is noticed in the early stages. If caught really early, it is sufficient to insert a special capsule that guards against timber rot. If the damage is a little more extensive, you will need to remove the damaged wood back to good timber and treat the gap with special timber rot compound. After the frame has been filled, planed, sanded and painted, nothing should be seen of the repair. If the rot is more extensive, you can limit the cost and retain the original window by removing and replacing just the sill and a small part of the stile (the most vulnerable areas).

ORIGINAL RAINWATER PIPES

Plastic guttering and downpipes can be replaced with iron, zinc or even copper pipes that are cast or extruded to original patterns. The hoppers at the top of the down pipes are also still available just as they used to be. Zinc and copper are expensive, but the scope in terms of size and dimensions is greater, and the life is longer, providing they are well maintained. Iron goods will last for decades, providing they are painted regularly. Maintenance-free PVC-u versions are available from specialist manufacturers in many period patterns and styles.

Lighting

As well as having an important practical function, lighting has an enormous influence on the style and character of each room of the home. Successful lighting needs to be planned at a very early stage in the design process, before the wiring has been installed (see the section on wiring on page 162). Do not forget to plan exterior lighting around the home and garden, too. This is important for safety and security, as well as making an attractive feature.

MAKE A LIST

The best electrical fittings do not get noticed. If there are sufficient power points, no trailing leads are needed. The best time to rewire is whilst alteration works are taking place. By making a check list for the alterations, you can prevent things having to be added or adapted later which could spoil your decorations. You may find it useful to make a scale plan of the room and draw out a wiring design. If you have already drawn up a plan to help you position your furniture, then you can add to this, placing light switches and sockets wherever they are required. Don't forget to add telephone and aerial points, or sockets for table lamps, the hi-fi, television and video. This is also the moment to arrange to lay loudspeaker cables out of sight. If you have furniture in the centre of a room and require a light, do not be afraid to place a power point in the floor, with a lid to conceal it when it is not in use. If you are rewiring, consider the position of the lighting; you do not just have to have a central pendant light. Consider spotlights, wall and table lights. You may choose to run more than one circuit, perhaps having a separate lighting circuit for ceiling, wall and table lights.

SPECIAL WISHES

On the resulting check list you can add the things you missed before: an additional light switch on the other side of the room; a telephone point or extra circuit in the kitchen; and a power point in the centre of the room, under the sofa or coffee table, for instance, for a standard lamp. Bear in mind the demands of modern equipment: where previously only a refrigerator and washing machine drew current, many homes now also have a microwave, a computer, a dryer, freezer and dishwasher, all demanding energy. Once you have a plan with all your wishes drawn on it, you can use this as the basis for obtaining estimates from some electricians. Ask for estimates from several firms because prices can vary widely.

STANDARD RULES FOR POWER POINTS

In principle, two power points are needed in each room or area of the home. Whenever the distance between points is greater than 3.5m (12ft), fix another double point between them just in case.

THE HEIGHT OF THE POWER POINTS

The power points in the corners of the room can be placed as low as possible so that little flex can be seen against the wall. Sometimes the local energy company stipulates a minimum height. This takes into account that the floors may be mopped, causing short circuits. Before you start your alterations, check with your electricity company what the rules are for your locality. For table lights, kitchen or computer equipment, it may be useful to place the power points at waist height. Those with mobility difficulties may also find waist height sockets more easily accessible.

CABLES OUT OF SIGHT

A power point in the floor with a metal lid can be an ideal solution for avoiding trailing leads. This earthed point is mounted in a metal housing and can be fixed to either wooden or concrete floors. Try to decide where the sofa or coffee table will be when carrying out alterations since this is often the most suitable place for a power point.

DIMMERS: LESS LIGHT, MORE ATMOSPHERE

Lower wattage lamps give a warmer light, but sometimes plenty of light is needed. A dimmer switch makes both possible. Nowadays many light fittings and lamps are sold with dimmers fitted to their leads. If not, this is easily arranged by replacing the existing switch with a dimmer. Standard dimmer switches cannot be used with halogen lamps that work with a transformer to lower the voltage; for instance, 12 volt halogen spotlights need a special dimmer. Halogen lamps that work at mains voltage and normal incandescent bulbs can, however, be controlled by the same standard dimmer. Energy saving lamps cannot be used with dimmers.

BASIC LIGHTING

Basic lighting does not have to mean a pendant light fixed in the centre of the ceiling. The main light switch can also control lighting for the dining table and various table or standard lamps. This creates a more intimate atmosphere when you turn on the lights.

LIGHTING WITH TWO FUNCTIONS

By fixing a dimmer to both the main and mood lighting, these lights can be used for both main illumination and mood setting. Uplighters – standard lamps directed towards the ceiling – light the ceiling more strongly, which gives an impression that it is higher.

FEATURE LIGHTING

For the lighting of paintings or still-lifes, for instance, feature lighting can be used. This can be done with spotlights built into the ceiling, surface mounted or mounted on track, or with a low-voltage cable system. To avoid pictures acting

as mirrors and to avoid shadows, feature lighting should be placed on the ceiling 80 to 120cm (32 to 48in) away from the wall. The higher the ceiling, the further from the wall the lights need to be fitted. Built-in spots, especially halogen, can be fitted only in lowered false ceilings. Take account of fire regulations, since halogen lamps give off lots of heat.

The bath-room

If you are rebuilding, remodelling, converting or building anew, then you will be able to design your bathroom with a clean sheet of paper. On your scale floor plan you will be able to try out several different combinations of sanitaryware in the same way as you did with your furniture. You can draw sanitaryware items as they would look from above, cut these out and then move them around your plan. Scale drawings of many models are now available in manufacturers' brochures. If you have the space, you can create an elegant bathroom designed for relaxation; but even a small bathroom has enormous scope with the right choice of bathroom and toilet fittings.

CHOOSING SLIMLINE SANITARYWARE

Before talking to the builder or plumber, draw up a list of the sanitary fittings that will be needed.

If there is not room for a bidet, separate shower, bath, double wash pedestals and a toilet, there are other convenient solutions. Baths combined with showers these days have good flat areas for showering, and there is a wide range of decorative shower panels and curtains from which to choose. There are also baths specially designed for smaller spaces. Instead of twin pedestals, two small basins that are sufficient for washing and shaving can be fitted in a counter. The toilet for the bathroom or cloakroom is

increasingly available in higher models. For a toilet that can be fitted at the height you prefer, there are suspended or wall-mounted models. These make it easier to clean the floor surrounding the toilet and also to keep the space looking less cluttered.

If space is very restricted, then a wet bathroom, where the room itself forms the shower enclosure, is the ideal solution. The walls and floor of such a bathroom are usually tiled and the floor slopes from the walls so that water drains into a central waste pipe.

A small downstairs cloakroom is a popular feature in many homes. The space under the stairs or an old cupboard may be the ideal location for

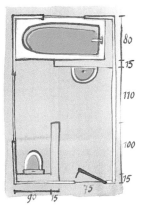

Partition walls permit separate toilet and shower corners.

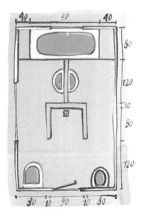

A central wall makes a shower and two washbasins possible.

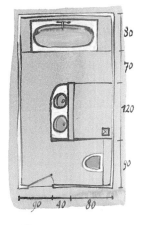

Plate glass and a partition wall form a shower area.

Annotated measurements are in centimetres: 90cm = 3ft

this. As when bathrooms have been added into other areas of the house, a small-bore waste pipe may be used in combination with a macerator and pump to avoid the need for a new soil stack.

COLOURED GLASS BUILDING BLOCKS

The layout of the bathroom can be made very interesting by the use of plain or coloured glass building blocks. They let light in for a spacious feeling and are available in a variety of finishes.

PARTITION WALLS

Bathroom fittings can be placed anywhere in the bathroom, even in the middle of the room, since free-standing partition walls can be constructed. Partition walls do not have to reach the ceiling: a height of just 120cm (4ft) means that washbasins can be hidden without making the space seem smaller. Additionally, the top of the wall can be used as a shelf or as the base for a free-standing mirror. A partition wall need not only be functional: it can also have an effect on the decorative scheme of the bathroom. Take the top of the partition wall as the

top line for the tiling to create a natural panelling. This can be made into a feature with the use of a line of different coloured border tiles.

TOILET: PLACE IT ANYWHERE

Partition walls make it possible for wiring and plumbing to be hidden from view, as the necessary ducts can be concealed in the void. The toilet can therefore be positioned wherever you want in the bathroom. Greater flexibility is offered by combination toilets that incorporate a pump to remove the waste. With these, the toilet can be placed some distance away from the soil pipe, or even in a basement.

WINDOW BLINDS FOR THE BATHROOM

The best blinds for the bathroom let light in by day and give privacy at night. They must be capable of withstanding excessive damp yet also be stylish. Stainless steel louvre blinds meet these

criteria. There are also various fabrics that are suitable for the bathroom. They can be used for both roller blinds and curtains. Make sure that the curtain rail or mounting system is moisture-resistant. The disadvantage of curtains is that they let in almost no light. Wooden blinds are also available in water-resistant timbers. Louvred shutters that fit to the inside of a window frame are another choice. Some types are adjustable to control the amount of light that is let in.

SAFETY IN THE BATHROOM

Anti-slip tiles are particularly important in the bathroom, especially if there are children or elderly people in the household. These are available in many colours and designs. There are even tiles designed specially for the 'children's bathroom'. If these are used together with a thermostatic shower control, then children can safely learn to take their first showers unaided, and

elderly people can retain their independence for longer. Consider, too, special corner mouldings that can be used to round off corners such as by the shower partition, so that no one risks cutting or bruising themselves. They are a delightful change from squared-off tiles.

LARGER THAN USUAL SHOWER-HEAD

Large shower-heads are currently very popular, as are special multi-function showers with multiple sprays and/or feature settings, like massage or steam. Such showers need to have a hot water system capable of delivering at least 16 litres (3½ gal) per minute. Once mixed with cold, that equals a fairly massive 25 litres (5½ gal) of warm water per minute. (By comparison, a normal shower uses 8–15 litres (1¾–3¼ gal per minute.) The same requirement applies if there are side sprays in addition to the main shower-head. A boiler with a minimum capacity of 150 litres (33 gal) is needed for these more complex showers.

THERMOSTATIC CONTROL

Because the thermostatic valve, once properly adjusted, automatically mixes water to the right temperature, it is both easy and safe for children to shower on their own. This is particularly useful in stopping a sudden blast of cold water when hot water is drawn somewhere else in the home.

THE FLOOR

Tiles and terrazzo have long been considered excellent bathroom materials for the floor, walls or vanity unit. They are particularly convenient for a wet bathroom (see page 167) because a drain can be included in such floors. With these materials, the bathroom and shower area can be seamlessly joined, with the shower floor slightly

lower so that it can be quickly dried with a sponge mop. The lack of edges and seams makes it easier to keep clean. Terrazzo comes in almost every colour and a range of finishes. It is laid and then polished *in situ*. Seamless bathrooms are also achievable with terrazzo, using smooth edging strips.

Wooden and laminate flooring is also now available for use in bathrooms, as are some types of stone and marble. Vinyl floors are popular and easy to keep clean. Finally, a cork-tiled floor can be made completely waterproof and will provide a warm and easily maintained floor-covering

A PLACE FOR THE WASHING MACHINE AND DRYER

The washing machine and dryer are often located in the kitchen, or a separate wash or utility room, positioned close to where washing can be hung out to dry. However, some owners prefer to install their washing machine and dryer upstairs near the bedrooms, where most of the dirty washing is generated. If the location is to be the bathroom, then the wiring for appliances has to be approved by an registered electrician in order to meet the strict safety requirements. See the illustration above and page 162 for information on installation.

HEATING IN THE BATHROOM

The central heating system can be used to supply under-floor heating for the bathroom as well as radiators and perhaps a heated towel rail. Under-floor heating is an ideal heat source for the bathroom. If you are not installing under-floor heating throughout the house, there are systems that can be added to a single room that hardly raise the floor level. Electrical heating or small-bore tubing of several millimetres can be laid under the floor. Another new alternative is mirror heating (not to be confused with mirrors that have a de-misting element fitted behind them). If the mirror is large enough (the installer can calculate this), the system can heat the entire bathroom. If the mirror is not large enough, a small decorative radiator or towel rail can be used as additional heating. If the bathroom has under-floor heating, a towel rail or radiator can still be run from the hot water supply, if it is a pumped system.

SMALL BATHROOM, SPACIOUS LAYOUT

If space is at a premium, then one way of making a bathroom seem larger is to place two washbasins with their backs to each other, each facing a partition wall about 170cm (67in) high (see illustration). This makes the bathroom seem wider than if the basins were placed next to each other.

Other ways of creating an impression of space

include carefully located mirrors, good lighting and light coloured walls.

VENTILATION

All 'wet' areas such as bathrooms need to be ventilated to prevent the build up of damp, stale air. Bathroom ventilation was traditionally provided by vents or open windows, but this has been replaced in modern homes by mechanical ventilation. Motorized fans located in an outside wall or window extract stale air, and fresh air is drawn in via vents. Bathrooms located away from external walls, for instance under the stairs, can be fittted with a duct to a remotely located extractor fan.

The kitchen

During the building or alteration of a kitchen it is often necessary to consider a wide range of issues. How often do you eat at home? How much space is needed for cooking? Does the whole family eat together? Do you want to be able to eat in the kitchen? Do you need wall cupboards or is there enough storage space in the base units? From the following information you can create a check list of all your needs.

CONSIDER THE LOCATION

When you have bought a new home or are intending to carry out extensive alterations, it seems obvious to leave the kitchen where it is because all the plumbing and wiring is there, and there are usually fitted units that might not take kindly to being ripped out of one room and reinstalled in another. However, if there are good reasons for wanting to move the kitchen from the back of the house to the front (often to achieve more and better light or to move to a larger room), it is possible, because the main gas, water and electricity connections are usually by the front door. Where you have an attractive rear garden there is a distinct advantage in such a move. The living room can be opened up across the entire width of the back of the house, and the addition of patio doors

opening onto the garden means that the garden can become part of the newly enlarged living room.

KEEP IT PRACTICAL

Before deciding on a kitchen it is important to think about how you use it. Do you mainly cook quick meals for two? If so, then a hob with four burners or rings and a microwave oven will do. If you like to cook in advance for the entire week, or regularly cook extensive dinners, think in terms of a wider hob, or one with variable rings that will take larger pans. You will also need a separate oven or one combined with a microwave. Having assessed your culinary lifestyle, make sure that there is room for a freezer of suitable capacity. The size of the kitchen has a bearing on the types of cupboard you should choose. Narrower kitchens are better with double

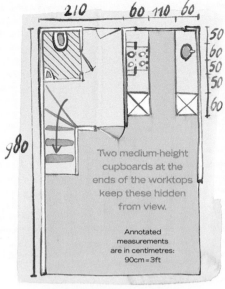

210   60   110   60

50 / 60 / 50 / 50 / 60

980

Two medium-height cupboards at the ends of the worktops keep these hidden from view.

Annotated measurements are in centimetres: 90cm = 3ft

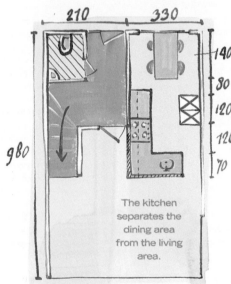

210   330

140 / 80 / 120 / 120 / 70

980

The kitchen separates the dining area from the living area.

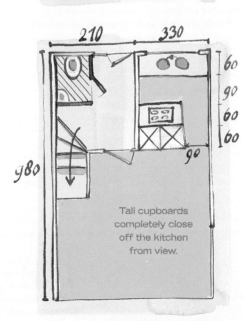

210   330

60 / 90 / 60 / 60

90

980

Tall cupboards completely close off the kitchen from view.

cupboard doors with a smaller opening radius of just 30cm (1ft). Finally, the refrigerator and freezer, hob and sink must be within easy reach of each other, without any obstructions.

Draw a plan of your ideas in order to visualize your kitchen, and try to imagine how it will look in three dimensions. The plan can bring to light various matters that need to be borne in mind. On which side of the refrigerator should the door open? How much room will there be to move around between the worktop and the kitchen appliances if they are installed as on the plan? An efficient kitchen is one where the cook can perform all the necessary tasks with the minimum of movement. So having the dishwasher near to the crockery cupboard and cutlery drawer will mean speedy unloading, and storing frequently used cooking ingredients near to the main worktop will avoid unnecessary fetching and carrying.

EXTRA SPACE

If you are remodelling, converting or building your own home, consider devoting some space to a separate utility room or even a walk-in pantry or food store. A utility room is the ideal spot for locating a deep-freezer, the washer/dryer, extra storage, the boiler and even the pet's basket.

POWER AND LIGHT

Following the instructions for drawing up a plan on page 162, you can make a plan of the new kitchen's electrical requirements. Firstly, there must be sufficient socket outlets for small appliances and fixed points for the main appliances. Four outlets in the wall is not extravagant luxury. They can also be positioned in the bottom of the wall units or in a drawer front. Remember that the washing machine should ideally be on a separate circuit and placed on a level floor. This might mean strengthening part of a wooden floor close to the outlet for the washing machine.

A golden rule for the kitchen is that nothing should block the path between the lighting and the work surface. The lighting therefore needs to be fixed as close to the work surface as possible. If there are no wall units, a cable can be installed above the worktop for halogen spotlights which give directable light. Spots with clamps that can be attached to shelves are a good alternative. Small fluorescent tubes were once widely used under wall units but there are now more attractive options. Halogen lights on a rail are very convenient because they can be moved at will. There are also extremely low-profile halogen spotlights that can be built into the underside of wall units.

WALL UNITS OR NOT?

A kitchen always seems bigger if there are no wall cupboards but not everyone has sufficient storage space without hanging units on the wall. If you need them but want to keep a sense of spaciousness, choose wall units with glass doors or with open shelves or racks. A stainless steel rod or rack on which you can hang meat cleavers, whisks and small pans is an attractive addition. Cupboards beneath the work surface can be more effectively used with slide-out racks or plenty of drawers, and turntables

OPEN-PLAN KITCHEN

If you have an open-plan kitchen in a room with an old timber floor but you want a different floor for the kitchen, you are immediately confronted with the problem of different levels. Even tiles and linoleum need board under them to prevent damage, which would result in a height increase of at least 2cm (¾in). An alternative is to screw a board or some rigid sheet material such as marine plywood to the floor. This can be painted and coated with clear varnish to provide a smooth, dirt-resistant floor.

for the corner units. Drawers can also be fitted in the plinth at the base of the cupboards, if it is made higher than usual.

CHANGING THE COLOUR OF YOUR KITCHEN

Do you want to change the colour of the cupboard fronts in your kitchen? If so, then there are several possibilities to consider:

■ If the doors and drawer fronts are of wood, degrease them well, sand them and paint them. Add two coats of varnish for protection against knocks and grease.

■ Plastic-coated cupboard fronts can be rubbed down with fine sandpaper or wire wool after they have been thoroughly cleaned. Coat them with an oil-based primer which provides a key for paint, then apply the paint of your choice – either oil- or water-based – on top. For fancy work, try your hand at some dragging or stippling, or opt for the fashionable distressed look by applying two coats of

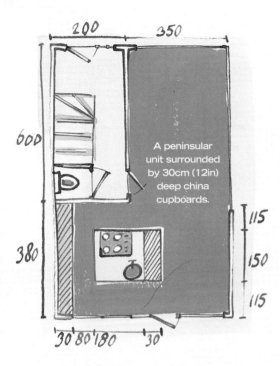

A peninsular unit surrounded by 30cm (12in) deep china cupboards.

paint and rubbing the top one away in places to reveal the underlying colour. Another idea is to use a fairly new product that produces a wood grain effect on non-wood surfaces. Once you have finished, either cover the decorated cupboard doors with two coats of varnish or take the doors to a paint sprayer who can coat them at the right temperature and pressure with hardened lacquer which will protect them against scratches and other marks.

■ Another possibility is to cover the doors with toughened plastic sheeting in a new colour. Get it done by a carpenter or furniture maker, because this is precision work. The cupboard hinges will need to be adjustable because the fronts will now be slightly thicker.

■ A metal worker or furniture maker can also cover them with stainless steel or zinc sheet for a thoroughly professional-looking kitchen.

WIDE RANGE OF WORKTOP MATERIALS

The choice of work surface will depend on its appearance, wear-resistance and, of course, the cost. Materials for work surfaces are available to suit every taste, but some are more easily damaged than others. Here is an overview of the main choices.

■ A terrazzo or granolithic finish is classical. The fragments of marble or granite can be given any colour. It is very hard wearing.

■ Wood is available with varnished or oiled finishes, but it needs regular

maintenance because any damage to the surface coating will make the wood porous. Laminate wood – a less expensive but more hard-wearing alternative to solid wood – is worth considering.

■ Artificial stone is a new material for the kitchen. Available in various designs and colours, it is heat resistant and does not crack.

■ Granite is suitable because of its hardness. It has beautiful natural figuring and colour. The surface withstands cracking and heat, but heavily coloured substances can stain it.

■ Plastic laminate worktops are available in a wide choice of designs and colours. Chemicals and acids do not damage them, but they are usually not completely heat resistant.

WALL BEHIND THE WORKTOP

New ideas for replacing tiles are constantly appearing on the market. A stainless steel panel to give an attractive and professional look to the kitchen, or plastic sheet glued to a board and then fixed to the wall are just two examples. Further ideas include a sheet of fibreglass or a plaster wall that has been decorated and then coated with a water-based varnish.

KITCHEN FLOORS

The choice for kitchen flooring is as broad as the

choice of work surface.

■ Linoleum offers a wide range of designs and colours. It needs a well-levelled base and for best results should be laid by a professional.

■ Stone slabs are dirt resistant because of their hard surface and also wear resistant. Stone is a timeless material that will last and last, but it needs to be laid on a solid floor base. Stone slabs can be either smooth, for a formal look, or uneven for a more rustic look.

■ Quarry tiles can be laid in attractive patterns. Their disadvantage is that they are porous and so are prone to staining unless waxed or treated regularly to keep them dirt resistant.

■ Laminated panels are available in various designs and colours. The better quality ones are suitable for the kitchen.

■ Wood or parquet creates a warm feeling but does not score so well in terms of resistance to water and dirt.

■ Marble and stone have a very long life, though marble needs a protective finish to avoid being stained.

■ Tiles are wear resistant and easy to keep clean. These hard flooring solutions such as stone and tiles are ideal for use with under-floor heating, which is the ideal heat source for a kitchen as it is both comfortable and unobtrusive.

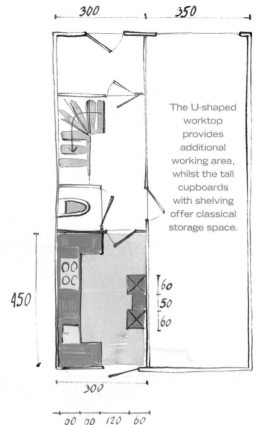

The U-shaped worktop provides additional working area, whilst the tall cupboards with shelving offer classical storage space.

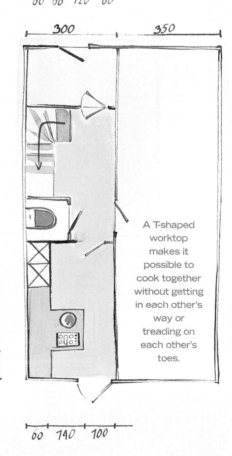

A T-shaped worktop makes it possible to cook together without getting in each other's way or treading on each other's toes.

Colour and paint

The easiest way to change the style of a home is to paint it. How you can achieve professional looking paintwork is dealt with here in this mini-course on painting.

EACH SPACE ITS OWN COLOUR

Most important when choosing colours is your personal preference. But the aspect of the room can also be an important consideration. The basic principal of using colour is that darker colours make a space or an object look smaller, whilst lighter hues have the opposite effect. Rooms facing north that never get any sun receive cool light. This can be countered by using warmer colours such as red, yellow, orange or shades of brown. Those that face south get masses of sunlight and benefit from softer shades that reflect less than white. Blue and green tints are not too cool to use in these circumstances and therefore work well.

CHOOSING COLOURS: PLAYING WITH EFFECTS

It is quite astonishing how different a room can look with the careful use of colour. The apparent breadth, height or length of a room can be influenced by it. A darker ceiling makes the room seem lower. If you need to increase the impression of height in a room, then the answer is to paint the ceiling lighter than the walls. Vertical stripes also create a sense of height. These can be in either contrasting colours or more muted self-stripes. The breadth of a room can be made to seem wider by using horizontal stripes. Finally, a large room can be made more intimate by painting the walls a darker colour. If you want colour but also the tranquillity of white, you can paint a 'panel' of colour or colourwash up to about 90cm (3ft) high, perhaps with a border, leaving the wall above this white. For a really restful room, paint the skirting-board the same colour as the lower part of the wall.

MINI-COURSE ON PAINTING

Once the colours have been chosen, the rest is down to your painting skills. Here are some tips.

1 ASSESSING WHAT NEEDS TO BE DONE

Whether the existing paint needs to be stripped completely depends upon its condition. Paintwork that is not more than two years old with little damage requires only sanding and cleaning. If there are cracks or blisters, you can check with a piece of adhesive tape how well the paint is adhering to the surface. Stick the tape on a weak patch and then remove it. If paint is left sticking to the tape, then the paint in that place needs to be stripped off. If more than 25 per cent is bad, it would be sensible to remove the lot.

2 GOOD TOOLS ARE HALF THE ANSWER

Old paint is removed using a sharp paint scraper or a filling or stripping knife. Make sure that the blade is smooth, because a rough blade might easily damage the surface of the wood. Besides the well-known triangular scraper for large surfaces, there are also various smaller scrapers for dealing with wooden mouldings (though anything delicate should be sanded instead). Burning off the paint can damage the timber and should never be done indoors. Much better is a heat gun which softens the paint, making it easier to remove. Paint strippers work efficiently but have the disadvantage that the wood has to be thoroughly cleaned and rinsed off afterwards. Strippers are quite corrosive and give off vapours that can be harmful if inhaled. It is best to avoid using them in poorly ventilated spaces or where there may be children present.

3 KNOTS CAUSE WEAK SPOTS

Paint does not adhere very well to knots or resinous wood. They are best dealt with by drilling them out or removing with a chisel. Knots from which resin weeps can sometimes be closed by heating them with a gas torch. Fill the holes with filler and, when dry, sand down to a level surface. Alternatively, knots can be sealed to prevent resin from bleeding from them and blistering the paintwork.

4 PREPARING FOR PAINTING

After the old paint has been removed, the condition of the wood can be assessed. If rot is discovered, small areas can be restored. Cut back the affected wood to sound timber and treat with wood preservative. Fill with a special filler. For larger areas, use a piece of Perspex (plexiglass) to stop the filler falling out before it has hardened. Place cling film (saran wrap) between the Perspex (plexiglass) and filler so that it can be removed easily when the filler is dry.

5 PROTECTING AGAINST ROT

The bottom corners of window and door frames are the most susceptible to rotting. Water becomes trapped in the cracks left when timber dries out. Rake this out to enlarge them and fill with a compound that remains elastic, such as a mastic sealer, and which can be painted over. Splits in window sills can be treated in the same way. Broken putty or window compound also lets in water. Replace the putty with glazing beads. Soften the existing putty with a heat gun to make it easier to remove. Smear a butyl glazing compound around the edge and push the beading into position. Fix it in place with small brads. Remove any excess compound. Cracked putty indoors can be handled in the same way.

6 RECOATING WOOD STAIN, EMULSION AND WHITEWASH

Wood stain only needs any loose flakes to be scraped off before it is re-coated. Sanding and cleaning is quite adequate.

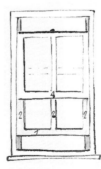 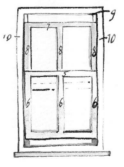

The numbering on the different types of window shows the ideal sequence in which to paint them. Make sure with sash windows that the sash cord does not get painted.

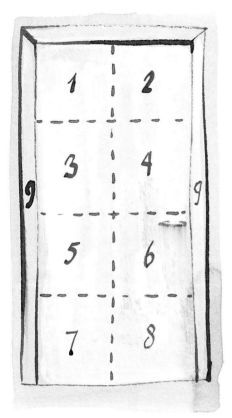

If you follow the numbered sequence shown for painting doors, you will achieve an attractive, even finish. This is particularly important with gloss paint. Laying off or brushing out the paint must be done, as far as possible, in only one direction.

Emulsion on walls and ceilings simply requires any cracks to be repaired before being wiped down with water to which a little ammonia has been added. It can then be re-painted. In older houses there may still be a layer of whitewash (a lime-based substance used for whitening walls, also known as distemper) on ceilings and walls. This cannot just be painted over because emulsion paint reacts with the lime in the whitewash, causing it to bubble and crack. Remove such a layer with a wet sponge and a filling knife or with wallpaper paste, which you paint on as thickly as possible and then brush off when it is almost dry. This is a convenient way to deal with mouldings and other ornamentation. If there appear to be remains of whitewash on a ceiling that you have just painted with emulsion, remove the patches, fill and then repaint them.

7 BEFORE YOU START PAINTING WOODWORK

Once the old or poor quality layers of paint have been removed, it is time to start rubbing down the woodwork. Use a fairly fine grade sandpaper for this to achieve a smooth surface. An electric sander gives the best results for relatively large, smooth areas, but always sand mouldings and beadings by hand or you might damage either the window pane or the moulding. Pine and teak both contain oily substances to which paint does not adhere easily, so these sorts of timber need to be thoroughly cleaned with ammonia or thinners before paint is applied.

8 PRIMING: THE FIRST LAYER

Bare wood that is to be painted must be primed first so that the top coats will key.
Where the wood is to be painted a dark colour, use a dark primer. The primer makes the wood fibres stand up so that the surface is made slightly rough. A light 'stroking' with sandpaper is sufficient to smooth this down and to help the next coat to hold. Always clean after sanding.
If you are painting wooden parts that are held together by tongue and groove, such as weather boarding or flooring on a veranda, it is best to prime the tongue and groove before assembling them because this protects them better against water. Any unevenness can then be made good with filler – indoors with special paint-like filler or quick filler (although this often cracks) and outdoors with liquid wood. Once this is dry, sand again with very fine grade paper. Clean the timber before painting so that it is smooth and free of grease. Wood stain does not need an undercoat, so the first layer is the stain itself.

9 CONDITIONS FOR THE FINAL COAT

When you apply the top coats the weather should be dry but not too warm. Never paint in full sun. Indoors make sure that everything that you paint is free from dust and grease. The first layer of the final coat never covers immediately. To prevent runs, apply two or more thin coats. Try to brush out (or lay) the paint in one direction, especially with gloss paint. If using a roller, run a brush just once lightly over the recently painted section to prevent air bubbles. Rub down lightly between each coat of paint and then clean and degrease before the next coat with water or ammonia. Finally, give horizontal parts of window frames a final coat. Wood stain always needs three coats for good cover. Paints are now available that include both primer and top coat in one, making painting woodwork faster and easier. These are available in matt, silk and gloss finishes. For a smooth, drip-free finish, these paints are still best applied in two or three thin coats.

MAINTAINING NEW PAINTWORK

It is important to clean paintwork regularly because this keeps the paint in better condition, reducing the frequency of repainting. Inspect paintwork every year for cracking, paying special attention to horizontal areas and the parts adjoining them. Gloss paint needs repainting about every six years; opaque stain about every four years, and transparent stain about every three years.

PAINTING METAL PARTS

Before painting pipes, radiators or metal staircase rails you must remove any rust. With new iron and steel, the blue/black layer needs to be removed because this prevents the paint from adhering well. Surface rust is removed with a steel brush; deeper rust requires emery paper or a sanding disc. After degreasing, give two coats of metal primer followed by two coats of paint.

Flooring

The choice of floor-covering has a tremendous impact on the style of a room, not only aesthetically in terms of its colour, pattern and surface texture, but also practically in terms of comfort and its feel underfoot. Whether you choose a soft or hard floor-covering depends upon the use of the room, the floor base and the position of the room in the home. Here is an overview of some of the options and the factors that might influence your selection.

TILES, TERRAZZO AND CEMENT FLOORS

A stone-type floor such as tiles, terrazzo or a fine-finish cement floor places an additional load on the floor which has to be considered. If the load is too great, the pressure on the sleeper walls may be too severe, causing cracking. The company supplying the flooring material can provide extensive information about the requirements for the floor base.

A stone floor is ideal for use with an under-floor heating system, which can reduce the number of radiators needed and so free valuable wall space for the furniture.

If you choose terrazzo or cement flooring that is to be coated, the floor needs to have an expansion joint – a small break that is filled with either plastic, aluminium, or a brass strip. This is necessary to permit the floor to expand when warm. Similar measures are also necessary for tiled floors, but the joints between

tiles provide the solution. In areas of less than 4 × 4m (13 × 13ft) this is not necessary. If you do not want a difference in levels and also wish to avoid over-stressing the construction of the floor, tiles can be laid on the

floor base. If you have a level concrete floor, tiles can be cemented directly to it with excellent results.

LAYING ONTO TIMBER

If you have a timber rather than a cement floor, you can successfully lay tiles on this too. Level the boards by screwing 18mm (¾in) thick marine plywood to the timber, preferably diagonally to the floor boards. Flat tiles can then easily be fixed to this surface.

FITTED CARPETS

The recent development of computer-controlled cutting techniques has significantly increased the ability to lay diverse patterns in carpet. By using two different colours of carpet, a neat stair runner can easily be created. For living rooms, a contrasting border is possible, or two different colours can be divided by a curved line

The advantage of carpet is that it diffuses light in a pleasing way, which is particularly useful for south-facing rooms. If you want to furnish your home with as little furniture as possible in rooms perhaps with high ceilings, fitted carpet can solve the problem of resounding noise.

QUALITY INFORMATION

Carpets have precise details about their suitability for different types of use clearly indicated in a standard quality system. The information on the back of the carpet helps you to choose the right carpet and indicates, for instance, if it is anti-static, and whether it is suitable for stairs or other main circulation areas, or only for use in bedrooms.

LAYING CARPET

The backing of the carpet determines how it is to be laid. There are textile-, foam- and latex-backed carpets. Only foam-

backed carpet can be laid without underlay directly on the floor with adhesive – although first laying hardboard is often advisable. In rooms up to about 16m² (19 sq. yd), carpet can be loose laid. In this case it is sufficient to stick the edges using double-sided carpet tape. If the backing is of textile or latex, an underlay is necessary. Normally such carpets are laid with tackless edging strips. When textile- or latex-backed carpets are laid without an underlay they are likely to wear badly. Without a springy underlay, they are also less comfortable to walk on. No underlay can be used with under-floor heating. The carpet must be stuck directly to the floor, which slightly reduces the efficiency of the heating.

THE PILE

Carpet comes in a wide assortment of types and lengths of pile. Whether the pile is open or closed depends upon how the knots are looped. If these are cut through, the pile sticks up to create open pile. Where the loops are not cut, they give the carpet a curly (or bouclé)

finish. The number of loops and the way they are attached to the backing determine the quality and price of the carpet.

VELVET EFFECT

Many open-pile carpets, such as velours, exhibit what is known as 'shading' – depending upon the direction of the pile, light is either reflected or absorbed, making the carpet seem darker or lighter, just like velvet. This is particularly noticeable after any vacuuming. If you wish to avoid this, examine carpet in a showroom from different angles and run your hand over the pile to judge the effect. Another way to avoid this phenomenon is to choose closed-looped carpets.

NATURAL FLOOR-COVERINGS

Floor-coverings made from natural fibres such as coir (coconut husk),

seagrass, sisal and jute are becoming increasingly popular, as their neutral shades work well with many styles of interior decor. The natural fibres are woven into coarse, hardwearing floor-coverings in a variety of textured patterns. Most natural floor-coverings are latex backed and so need to be used in conjunction with an underlay. Fitting techniques are the same as for carpet and other soft floor-coverings.

LAYING CARPET YOURSELF

Before laying carpet, the floor must be dry, level, firm and smooth. With timber floors, that usually means laying hardboard or chipboard. Any gaps or cracks in a concrete floor must be filled before the carpet is laid.

Carpet is usually laid with adhesive or stretched (work for a craftsman). Special environmentally friendly adhesives without solvents are available for gluing carpets.

Where carpet meets other floor-coverings it should be terminated with a strip that looks neat and protects it from wear. Two different carpets are joined with a tackless edging strip. These are strips with hooks on that are fixed to the floor, to hold the carpet. Special edge profiles are used to finish the carpet off neatly where it borders a smooth floor such as wood.

LOOKING AFTER CARPET

For stains use clean hand-hot water with a few drops of washing-up liquid. Carbonated water is a good alternative – the bubbles work in the same way as the washing-up liquid. Stain removers or collar and cuff washing bars or liquids can also be used, but do not use too much. Work from the edge to the middle of the stain, dabbing, not rubbing, then rinse with a little water. Stains in sisal floor-covering can be removed with a brush and luke-warm water with a little ammonia. Chewing gum is removed from carpet and sisal by first cooling it with ice blocks or gas from a lighter refill.

VINYL FLOOR-COVERING

Vinyl-covered floors are easy to keep clean and can be very inexpensive. For vinyl to stay looking good though it needs a completely smooth base. Laying vinyl yourself is relatively easy but preparing the right base is far more trouble and usually demands a craftsman's skills. If laying vinyl yourself, work from the centre of the room. Lay the surplus up over the skirting and smooth the vinyl out towards the edges. Fold the excess back double against the skirting and cut with a sharp craft knife or similar. Cut slightly above the fold for the right size. If you cut on the fold line the vinyl will be slightly too short. Practice with an off-cut so that you can get used to where to cut. If the vinyl bubbles up, you have not cut off enough. Lay a ruler along the skirting and cut a small additional amount off. A couple of millimetres is usually enough.

LINOLEUM AND SIMILAR FLOORING

The laying of linoleum and other similar flooring material is work for a specialist. The substrate must be completely level and smooth before laying. Solid floors are levelled using a near-liquid levelling compound. Timber floors are prepared with a rigid board or sheet material of 18 to 22mm (¾ to ⅞in) thickness. Beautiful patterns can be formed with linoleum, using repeating patterns, edge designs, wavy borders, and even totally contrasting colours. When this type of flooring is laid in damp rooms, it is important that the seams are welded. When the floor has been laid, it is coated with a protective layer, because linoleum is not water-resistant. A water-resistant treatment should be applied twice a year. Cleaning is quite easy – vacuum and mop with a well-wrung out mop, using water with a little floor cleaner added.

LAMINATED FLOOR

Laminated floor is a relatively new type of flooring. Its great advantages are that it is an extremely convenient flooring, which is easy to lay yourself, can be much cheaper than solid timber floors, is colour-fast and its top layer is extremely tough and wear resistant (unlike the varnish layer of parquet). It is made of laminations of different materials: a damp-proof layer, a thin board, a thin layer with a photographic print of wood grain and finally an extremely hard clear plastic layer. Laminated flooring is available in various sizes, depending upon the manufacturing process, (20 × 20 cm, 20 × 60cm and 20 × 120cm/8 × 8in, 8 × 24in and 8 × 48in). The edges are tongued and grooved. Laminated sections are laid on a level floor. Glue is applied to the grooves and then the sections are pressed together firmly. Laminated floor can be laid virtually anywhere in the home, even on top of old carpet or other floor-coverings.

VARIOUS DESIGNS

Laminated flooring is available in a very wide choice of colours and designs, making it possible to combine different finishes together, such as a dark wood finish passageway in the hall with borders in a lighter wood finish that is then used in neighbouring rooms. Alternatively, a patterned border may be used to mark off the seating area or another part of the floor covered with a different design. Maintaining laminated floors is an easy matter. The tough top layer is both dirt and water resistant. Vacuuming and an occasional going over with a mop are sufficient. A sponge floor mop with interchangeable heads is useful and can be quicker than a vacuum cleaner.

Spots such as grease, chocolate or wine can be removed with hot water and a gentle detergent. More stubborn stains such as shoe scuffs, cigarette marks, tar or soot should be cleaned with acetone or methylated spirits. Pencil can simply be rubbed out.

TIMBER FLOORS

The various types of wooden floor (boards, solid parquet or laminated parquet) have more or less the same properties. The base for these wooden floors has to be level, and timber can be laid on a solid floor.
Floating laminated timber floors, which are not fixed down but are laid directly on top of existing flooring, or on special felt, are becoming popular. If you select such a 'floating' floor, a lightly sprung layer is first rolled out across the floor and the timber is laid on top of this. This layer slightly deadens the sound and evens out any minor irregularities in the floor.

The parquet sections or boards are then fitted together with their tongues and grooves. Special edging strips keep the loose laid floor in place. A small expansion gap of a few millimetres is left around the edge of the room between the wall and the wooden floor, hidden under the skirting-board or a strip of wood. This will prevent the floor from lifting in warm, humid conditions.
There is another system with which the sections are held together with sprung metal clips. With this type it is even possible to take the floor with you when you move.
For a fixed floor on a solid base, chipboard must first be laid to form a base. Bear in mind any wiring or plumbing under the floor. In many new homes, central heating and water pipes and electric cables are run under concrete floors. Once this is fixed firmly in place, the wooden floor can be nailed or glued to

LAMINATED FLOORING IN AN APARTMENT

Footsteps and moving furniture can cause noise problems for downstairs neighbours if you live in an apartment with laminated flooring. Sound-deadening laminated flooring is available that will help overcome this problem. Both the bottom and surface layers are made of fibres that absorb the sound so that it is not transmitted through the floor.

the chipboard base. If a wooden floor is to be laid on top of a timber floor, it is straightforward. Finally, it is possible to use the existing timber boards as flooring if it is in good condition, or it can be restored (see section on repairing and restoring wooden floors, page 163). Check the entire floor for nails and screws from previous floor-coverings before sanding. The floor can be as good as new after running over it with a floor sander and treating it with a floor finish. Bear in mind that any neighbours downstairs will have problems with noise if their ceiling is right below your floor.

VARNISH OR WAX?

The finishing of a floor can be done in a number of ways. It can be painted or stained to alter its colour and appearance, and varnished, treated with oil or wax polished to protect it and give it a shine. Which is best depends upon the use of the room and your personal preference. Polishing with wax needs doing more often than varnishing, as does the application of other soft finishes, such as oil. Some oil and wax polishes are available with stains mixed in to save having to apply colour separately. Varnishes, too, are available with colour stains. Varnish is best in several coats and will give a harder wearing finish;

however, it can be prone to scratching or cracking, especially from furniture, and these marks are harder to remove than with wax. Gloss varnish can also look less cosy than wax.

With all types of stain or wood dye, any remaining paint or varnish needs to be fully removed in order to achieve an even finish, and at least three coats of stain or dye are required. The alternatives are almost endless. It is also possible to buy ready-finished timber flooring that can be walked on as soon as it is laid.

MAINTENANCE

Maintenance of impregnated or waxed floors consists mainly of vacuuming and mopping. Special parquet mops for use with a vacuum cleaner can be bought from companies that supply parquet. The layer of wax needs to be as thin as possible because thicker layers quickly become dirty. A further coating of wax is only needed when the floor is really bare of wax, and even then only the worn areas should need treating.

With a varnished floor the daily cleaning consists only of vacuuming. Stains can usually be cleaned off with a damp cloth. There are various cleaning agents available from chemists or parquet flooring companies for treating more stubborn stains on these floors.

The open fire

Open fires create a cosy atmosphere in the home. Regardless of whether the fireplace is a minimalist hole in a wall or a more grand affair built of sandstone with an antique surround, it is the size of the chimney that determines how well the fire burns.

Almost every type of open fire can be built into a home, though in some circumstances the design of the chimney will have to be adapted. Older houses usually have a fireplace, but these are often designed for oil- or gas-burning stoves. The diameter of the flue for these is much smaller than that needed for an open fire. Generally, an open fire needs a flue no smaller than 20cm (8in). A fireplace installer or chimney sweep can assess your existing chimney. If there is no chimney it can be made using double-walled stainless steel tubing which is joined together with spring clips. The smooth inside of the flue ensures that the fire draws well. The system is available in various diameters. The right diameter depends upon the size of the fireplace. New ducted flues can often be fitted in existing chimneys. The flue needs to be as straight as possible and should have the same diameter throughout. The material has to cope with steam that condenses, and insulation is important to prevent the flue from cooling too quickly.

UNUSUALLY SHAPED HEARTHS

For a hearth of unusual dimensions or with an unusually shaped opening, the fireplace needs to be built of firebricks, using fireproof mortar. With these materials, any form of fireplace that is wanted can be constructed. It is more usual, however, for people to select a standard hearth, with a hood of wrought iron or of special fire-resistant concrete. There is little difference in the quality.

FIRE GRATE OR DOGS

It looks attractive to see the fire laid directly on a fireproof hearth, but if the fire will not burn very well, fire dogs might be the solution. Logs are placed on the fire dogs, which leaves room beneath for the ashes and embers. This makes it

> ### START EARLY
> The desire to create an open fireplace often happens in the autumn. Remember, however, that it can take months before a new fireplace can be lit for the first time because the construction has to harden. It is best dealt with by a specialist and started in the summer.

Grilling on charcoal between the kitchen and dining room.

An attractive fireplace also adds style in the summer months.

easier to clean the fire. If you do not succeed with your first attempts to light a fire, there are specially made logs of pressed timber available that make it child's play.

VENTILATION WITH OPEN FIRES

Open fires use up lots of oxygen. This is drawn from the living area, making ventilation essential. It is possible, of course, to leave a window ajar, but this would largely negate the point of lighting the fire in the first place. More comfortable alternatives are to have special ventilation grills built into the windows or airbricks placed at skirting height. These have the advantage of not causing a draught whilst ensuring that the fire burns well.

ADJUSTING THE THERMOSTAT

By burning an open fire, the temperature in the room will rise and, if the main thermostat is located in the vicinity, the central

heating will switch itself off. The temperature elsewhere in the house will therefore become colder. This can be avoided by fitting individual thermostatic valves to the radiators so that the temperature of each room can be individually set. This will increase the energy efficiency of the heating system. If you retain the use of a main thermostat, cite it as far away from the fireplace as possible, perhaps choosing the hall or dining-room as a more suitable location.

CARE WITH STOKING

To limit environmentally harmful waste products, it is best to stoke the fire with only dry, unpainted timber. Well-dried wood burns better, gives more heat, pollutes less and creates less soot in the chimney. Do not stoke the fire when it is foggy or there is no wind. The chimney will not draw properly in this sort of weather and the fire will not burn properly. In addition, the smoke will probably hang in the air. Generally speaking, you can reckon that the lighter coloured the smoke is, the cleaner the fire is burning.

OPTIMUM BURNING OPEN FIRE

A fire will not burn well with a chimney that does not draw properly. In such cases a flue glass ventilator that mechanically draws the flue gases upwards into the chimney is the solution. The equipment is placed in the chimney and is fully adjustable so that the precise draught can be created. They are available in models for both circular and rectangular section chimney flues, and for brick or metal flues. More information is available from a fireplace installer, a chimney sweep, or from manufacturers.

THE CHIMNEY: SWEEP AT LEAST ONCE A YEAR

Get a chimney sweep to clean the chimney before the start of the open fire season. A fire will burn properly only if the chimney is kept swept. The sweep can check the condition of the flue and trace any leaks.

ANTIQUE FIREPLACES

Old fireplaces are becoming increasingly popular and can be found at architectural salvage yards. Although in general the older the fireplace, the greater the value, fireplaces from some periods are less popular than others and the price will reflect this. Before installing an old fireplace, first make sure that it complies with today's safety regulations. Antique fireplaces are usually ideal for wood or other solid fuel fires, as this was what they were originally designed for, but some can also be adapted for real flame effect fires using propane or natural gas. Another option is to buy a reproduction fireplace from the wide range currently available.

The side of the chimney makes a fine cupboard.

The attic

The attic in many houses is frequently used for little more than storing unused items. Yet this space can quite easily be given a better use: perhaps as an extra bathroom, a work room or study, a separate floor for an au pair, or somewhere to lay out the trainset. If an attic is to be used as a bedroom or living area it must be well ventilated and have sufficient daylight. Thorough insulation will be necessary to keep out the cold in winter and the heat in summer.

FIRST INSULATE

Before converting or re-arranging the attic, it is sensible to insulate it. See 'Insulation' on page 164 to find out how this can be done. Once the roof area has been insulated, you have a choice of ways to finish the ceiling and walls. For a rustic or natural effect you can use tongued and grooved boards. Finally, you can paint or stain the timber, to your personal choice. If you decide upon plaster-board, the ceiling and walls can be plastered, painted or papered.

DORMER WINDOW

If the attic is somewhat small and dark, consider having a dormer built. Depending upon the existing space, this can provide a great deal more space (see illustration). Before making any alterations to the structure or appearance of your property, check that there are no restrictions or requirements imposed by the local authorities. Obtaining permission to make changes to buildings of historic importance or character may be difficult.

STANDARD OR MADE-TO-MEASURE

Dormer extensions are available in prefabricated form from various manufacturers. For the design of a bespoke dormer, an architect, building surveyor or structural engineer are the appropriate professionals. They will draw the dormer that fulfils your

Attic space without dormer window.

Extra headroom with dormer window.

A partition wall with shelving provides extra storage

wishes and suits the style of your home. Once your chosen professional has prepared detailed plans, these can be used as the basis to obtain quotations from contractors. It may be convenient to ask your local contractor because they are likely to be aware of the local regulations. Always make sure that the contractor you appoint has experience in handling similar work for other people. It is always sensible to ask for references and to check that previous clients were satisfied with their work.

WINDOWS

With one or more windows in the roof you can get masses of natural light in the attic. Roof windows are available in different types. The best known are the pivoting windows that are hinged in the middle. Where there is little headroom, a window hinged at the top may be preferable. An unusual type is the so-called balcony window. This consists of two windows on top of each other in the sloping roof. The upper window is hinged at the top while the lower window is hinged at the bottom. The upper window opens to an almost horizontal position, the lower one to a vertical position. With a special fence on the side, it creates a 'balcony'.

EXTRA BATHROOM

An additional bathroom in the attic requires special considerations to deal with dampness. Particular considerations will be ventilation and the location of the plumbing. A combination system with a macerator and pump will allow the toilet to be located in any position, without the need for a new soil stack. The pump may also be able to pump away waste from the sink, shower or bath. For information on ventilating bathrooms, see page 169. Another factor to bear in mind is the strength of the attic floor, and whether this will need additional support to cope with the extra weight.

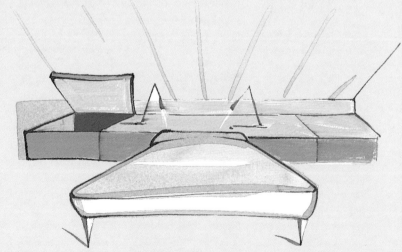

Where the ceiling is too low for seating, you can make extra storage space.

CONCEALING APPLIANCES

Some homes may have a cold water storage or header tank in the attic. This can usually be moved to a different, more convenient spot, or a partition wall can be built to screen the tank. Such a wall has the added advantage of creating extra storage space because shelves can be mounted on both sides of the wall. Alternatively, the tank can be done away with altogether through the installation of a mains pressure plumbing system. This is only possible in areas where there is sufficient mains water pressure.

CREATING STORAGE SPACE IN THE ATTIC

Whilst the benefit of converting an attic is to provide extra sleeping or living space, the downside can be a loss of storage space. With good design, however, it is possible to maintain considerable storage space by building cupboards around the chimney breast or where the roof slope begins to meet the floor.
A high roof offers the scope for adding an additional floor between the ridge and the attic floor. This new loft can provide space to store things not in everyday use. This is a job for a professional because the roof must be able to bear the load of the new floor and storage.

COMPARE FIRST
Both professionals and builders have their own terms and prices. Therefore you should ask for several estimates to compare before choosing. Confirm any agreements in writing, as far as possible, to prevent any problems later.

REPLACING TRUSSES
If your attic structure has lots of supports at eye level, it is possible to remove these so that you can stand upright, provided that additional support is created elsewhere. This is work for a professional or specialist contractor, because the forces on the roof and walls have to be calculated. If the floor of your attic has not been built to be used as a room, the beams will need to be strengthened, supported or replaced.

Security

Protecting your home against burglars is not just a matter of good locks. Deterring burglars in the first place is vital, so consider installing a burglar alarm or lights that come on when movement is detected. Good lighting in the garden and by entry points can also be a deterrent.

QUALITY LOCKS

Do not choose lower quality locks for doors that are out of sight. Back doors are more at risk of a break-in than front doors. Old houses often have locks with simple lever locks. Such locks are easily opened. Replace these as first priority with cylinder locks.

SECURE EVEN THE SMALLEST VENT

The windows as well as the doors may need to be fitted with locks. Even the smallest window vent can be useful for the housebreaker. Surface locks, which are easy to fit yourself, are available for windows and shutters that open outwards. Locks for building into the frame are more suitable for windows that open both inwards and out. The window locks should also be capable of being opened with one key for safety reasons.

ONE KEY, MANY LOCKS
When there are a number of outside doors, including the garage and shed, it is useful to have one key to fit all the outside doors. Have locks fitted that can all be opened with the same key, doing away with the bunch of keys.

MORTISE BOLTS ARE ESSENTIAL

In addition to good locks, the hinges play a security role. Mortise bolts can be combined with the hinge. They connect the door and frame together so that the door is harder to force open and cannot be lifted off its hinges.

FITTING LOCKS: A CRAFT

It is best for locks to be fitted by a specialist, even for the good do-it-yourselfer. Some firms will come to give free advice on security matters and estimates. The type of locks that you have installed may be taken into account by your household contents insurer. Good locks may result in a reduction in your premium.

EXTRA SECURE: A SAFE

A safe can be used for many things. Firstly, of course, it is useful for protecting valuables such as jewellery and cameras. But passports and insurance policies also deserve a safe place. Many safes also provide fire protection for important documents.

TYPES OF SAFE

There are furniture safes, wall safes and floor safes. A safe is of value only if it is firmly anchored to the fabric of the house. Security experts can advise. They can also arrange to install the safe. Insurance companies sometimes insist that valuables are kept in a safe, although they may require the safe to be installed by the supplier.

LIGHTING AS DETERRENT TO BURGLARS

Lighting that scares off burglars is available in various types. One of the best known is the lamp with a movement detector

Cylinder locks are more secure than simple lever locks.

Anti break-in strip for an inward opening door.

Anti break-in strip for an outward opening door.

The most secure method: the screws are hidden.

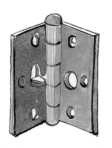

A hinge with a break-in resistant stud.

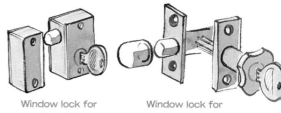

Window lock for surface fixing.

Window lock for mortise fitting.

SECURITY GADGETS

Video intercoms are now available that allow homeowners to see and talk to visitors at the gate or front door before answering. These systems can even be connected to a spare channel on a television set. As prices fall, remote cameras, linked to the video for when no one is at home, are likely to be an increasingly popular feature of home security systems.

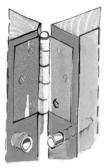

The pin ensures that the door cannot be forced off its hinges.

which goes on if anyone moves within the beam from the sensor. These are particularly useful installed near the front door, because they are helpful to the householder hunting for keys at night and also illuminate a potential entry point for the would-be burglar. One sensor can control a number of lamps. These are available at do-it-yourself stores, builder's merchants, garden centres and lighting shops.

ALTERNATIVE: THE PHOTO-ELECTRIC CELL

Movement detectors have the disadvantage that they can react to moving animals or, during stormy weather, to leaves and branches. If you find it a distraction to have the lights going on and off, there is an alternative. This is to control the lights with a photo-

electric cell which will switch the lighting on at dusk and off at dawn.

INTERIOR LIGHTING

There are variations on this theme available for interior use too. Timer devices that plug into household sockets, and into which lamps are then plugged, can be set to go on and off so that the house looks occupied. You can purchase either a simple 24-hour timer or a more sophisticated seven-day version. Other similar devices turn on at dusk and off at dawn, whilst others still are noise-sensitive. So a knock or ring at the door will result in a light going on. Of course, not only lamps can be plugged into these timers: a radio or television could be used instead to give the impression that the house is occupied.

ALARMS

If all the other security systems are not sufficient, you can have an alarm system installed. Some set off flashing lights and sirens. The would-be burglar is usually long gone before the police are called. The alarm can be connected to a private alarm control centre. The people who work there can see from a code where the break in is happening and warn the police or a security firm. Such systems can be silent or coupled to a lamp and siren. The installation of alarms and other security systems may reduce the cost of home insurance.

HOW DOES AN ALARM SYSTEM WORK?

Infra-red movement detectors are installed at key places around the home and linked to each other and the alarm unit by wires. These detectors may be combined with pressure mats or switches that are triggered when certain doors or windows are opened. All of these items are linked together and any one of them may trigger the alarm.

Many alarms also have panic buttons located at strategic positions, such as by the front door and master bed.

By means of a code or a key, the system can be switched on or off at the control unit, although remote controlled units are also available. Some systems are designed to scare burglars or to warn the occupants or their neighbours of intrusion. Maintenance and service costs have to be paid for systems that are connected to a central control.

Window catches with locks are also safer for children in high-rise apartments.

Mortise bolts can be fitted to frames, and screws can be replaced with mortise bolts on the other side of the window too. If the window opens, fix an anti break-in strip.

WIRELESS ALARM SYSTEMS

Installing a conventional alarm system into an existing property can disturb the decoration and building fabric, as the wiring needs to be concealed for security. This disturbance is not a problem where renovation, building or redecoration work is taking place, but can be avoided by installing a wireless alarm system. As with a conventional alarm, there is a combination of infra-red movement detectors, pressure mats, etc., but these are all connected by coded radio signals rather than by wires and are powered by battery. Only the control station and alarm unit need to be powered from the mains (although they have a battery back-up in case of power failure). This sort of system is relatively easy to install on a DIY basis and can prove very cost effective.

Useful addresses

ANTIQUE AND SALVAGE BUILDING MATERIALS

Dorset Reclamation
Cow Drove
Bere Regis
Wareham
Dorset BH20 7JZ
Tel: 01929 472200

London Architectural Salvage & Supply Company (LASSCo)
St. Michael's Church
Mark Street
London EC2A 4ER
Tel: 0171 739 0448

Salvo
Ford Woodhouse
Berwick-upon-Tweed
TD15 2QF
Tel: 01668 216494

Walcot Reclamation
108 Walcot Street
Bath BA1 5BG
Tel: 01225 444404

BESPOKE KITCHENS

A. Bell & Company Ltd
Kingsthorpe Road
Northampton
NN2 6LT
Tel: 01604 712505

AEG (UK) Ltd
55–77 High Street
Slough
Berkshire SL1 1BF
Tel: 01753 872299

Alno Ltd
Unit 10, Hampton
Farm Industrial Estate
Hampton Road West
Hanworth
Middlesex TW13 6DB
Tel: 0181 898 4781

Alternative Plans
9 Hester Road
London SW11 4AN
Tel: 0171 228 6460

Robert Bosch Domestic Unit Ltd
Grand Union House
Old Wolverton Road
Wolverton
Milton Keynes
MK12 5PT
Tel: 01895 838383

Care Design
Moorgate
Ormskirk
Lancashire L39 4RX
Tel: 01695 579061

Franke UK Ltd
East Park, Manchester
International Office
Centre
Styal Road
Manchester M22 5WB
Tel: 0161 436 6280

The Kitchen People
37 Wigmore Street
London W1H 9LD
Tel: 0171 495 3663

Magnificent Marble
276 High Street
Sutton
Surrey SM1 1PG
Tel: 0181 643 1723

Plain English
Tannery, Combes
Stowmarket
Suffolk
IP14 2EN
Tel: 01449 774028

SieMatic Mobelwerke GmbH & Co
Osprey House
Rookery Court
Primett Road
Stevenage
Hertfordshire
SG1 3EE
Tel: 01438 369251

Smallbone & Co (Devizes) Ltd
The Hopton
Workshop
London Road
Devizes
Wiltshire
SN10 2EU
Tel: 01380 729090

Mark Wilkinson Furniture Ltd
Overton House
High Street
Bromham
Chippenham
Wiltshire
SN15 2HT
Tel: 01380 850004

Whitton Wood Designs
37 Crown Road
St. Margaret's
Twickenham
Middlesex
TW1 3EJ
Tel: 0181 891 6639

Woodstock
4 William Street
Knightsbridge
London
SW1X 9HL
Tel: 0171 245 9989

Zeyko Kitchens
The Business Design
Centre
52 Upper Street
Islington
London N1 0HQ
Tel: 0171 288 6123

BLINDS AND SHUTTERS

American Shutters
72 Station Road
London
SW13 OLS
Tel: 0181 876 5905

The Blinds Company
Unit 2
London Stone
Business Estate
Broughton Street
London SW8 3QR
Tel: 0171 627 0909

Olivia Brett
Puck Mill Farm
Frampton Mansell
Gloucestershire
GL6 8JQ
Tel: 01285 760402

The Louvre Blind Company Ltd
1 Forward Drive
Harrow
Middlesex HA3 8NT
Tel: 0181 863 9111

The Shutter Shop
Queensbury House
Dilly Lane
Hartley Wintney
Hampshire
RG27 8EQ
Tel: 01252 844575

Swift Blinds
Aldon Manufacturing
(Huddersfield) Ltd
Aldon Works
177 Lockwood Road
Huddersfield HD1 3TG
Tel: 01484 513608

Technical Blinds Ltd
Tusthorn Avenue
Coleford
Gloucestershire
GL16 8PR
Tel: 01628 530511

DOORS, HINGES AND DOOR FURNITURE

G. & S. Allgood Ltd
297 Euston Road
London NW1 3AQ
Tel: 0171 387 9951

Any Old Iron
PO Box 198
Ashford
Kent TN26 3ZT
Tel: 01622 685336

Sabrina Oak Doors
Alma Street
Mountfields
Shrewsbury
Dorset SY3 8QL
Tel: 01743 357977

N. T. Yannedis & Co Ltd
Riverside House
Southend Road
Woodford Green
Essex IG8 8HQ
Tel: 0181 550 8833

FABRICS AND UPHOLSTERY

Manuel Canovas Ltd
2 North Terrace
Brompton Road
London SW3 2BA
Tel: 0171 225 2298

The Conran Shop
81 Fulham Road
London SW3 6RD
Tel: 0171 589 7401

The Curtain Shop
54 Abbey Gardens
London NW8 9AT
Tel: 0171 372 1044

Fabric World
6-10 Brighton Road
South Croydon
Surrey CR2 6AA
Tel: 0181 688 6282

Habitat
196 Tottenham Court
Road
London WIP 9LD
Tel: 0171 255 2545

**JAB International
Furnishings Ltd**
1/15-16 Chelsea
Harbour Design
Centre
Chelsea Harbour
London SW10 OXE
Tel: 0171 349 9323

**John Lewis
Partnership**
278-306 Oxford Street
London W1A 1EX
Tel: 0171 629 7711

Liberty
214 Regent Street
London W1R 6AH
Tel: 0171 734 1234

Monkwell Ltd
10-12 Wharfdale Road
Bournemouth
Dorset BH4 9BT
Tel: 01202 762456

The Natural Fabric Co
Wessex Place
127 High Street
Hungerford
Berkshire RG17 ODL
Tel: 01488 684002

Osborne & Little
304 King's Road
London SW3 5UH
Tel: 0171 352 1456

Classic Silks
140 Watlington Road
Runcton Holme
King's Lynn
Norfolk PE33 OEJ
Tel: 01553 810604

VV Rouleaux
10 Symons Street
London SW3 2TJ
Tel: 0171 730 4413

FLOOR-COVERINGS AND CARPETS

The Amtico Co Ltd
Kingfield Road
Coventry CV6 5PL
Tel: 01203 861400

Bronte Carpets Ltd
Bankfield Mill
Greenfield Road
Colne
Lancashire BB8 9PD
Tel: 01282 862736

**Christopher Farr
Handmade Rugs**
115 Regent's Park Road
London NW1 8UR
Tel: 0171 916 7690

Crucial Trading
79 Westbourne Park
Road
London W2 4BX
Tel: 0171 221 9000

Elon
66 Fulham Road
London SW3 6HH
Tel: 0171 460 4600

Fired Earth
Twyford Mill
Oxford Road
Adderbury
Oxfordshire OX17 3HP
Tel: 01295 812088

Hugh Mackay Carpets
PO Box 1
Durham City
County Durham
DH1 2RX
Tel: 0191 386 4444

LTP
Tone Industrial Estate
Milverton Rd
Wellington
Somerset TA21 OAZ
Tel: 01823 666213

Natural Carpets
Talent House
Chorlton
Hampshire SP10 4AX
Tel: 01264 336845

FLOORS – STONE AND TERRAZZO

Classical Flagstones
Lyncombe Vale Farm
Lyncombe Vale
Bath BA2 4LT
Tel: 01225 316759

European Heritage Ltd
48-52 Dawes Road
London SW6 7EJ
Tel: 0171 381 6063

**Granite Marble
& Stone Ltd**
Unit 7, Crown Yard
Bedgebury Road
Goudhurst
Kent TN17 2QZ
Tel: 01580 212222

Naturestone
The Design Village
Crossways
Silwood Road
Sunninghill
Ascot
Berkshire SL5 OPZ
Tel: 01344 27617

Paris Ceramics
583 King's Road
London SW6 2EH
Tel: 0171 371 7778

Reed Harris
27 Carnworth Road
Fulham
London SW6 3HR
Tel: 0171 736 7511

Stone Age Ltd
19 Filmer Road
London SW6 7BU
Tel: 0171 385 7954

Stonnell
Bockingfold
Ladham Road
Goudhurst
Kent TN17 1LY
Tel: 01580 211167

FLOORS – TILES AND MOSAIC

Attica
543 Battersea Park Road
London SW11 3BL
Tel: 0171 738 1234

Fired Earth
Twyford Mill
Oxford Road
Adderbury
Oxfordshire OX17 3HP
Tel: 01295 812088

Pilkington's Tiles Ltd
PO Box 4
Clifton Junction
Manchester M27 8LP
Tel: 0161 727 1000

Siesta Cork Tiles Ltd
Unit 21
Tait Road
Croydon
Surrey CRO 2DP
Tel: 0181 683 4055

Terra Firma Tiles
70 Chalk Farm Road
London NW1 8AN
Tel: 0171 485 7227

FLOORS – WOOD

Finewood Floors
5 Gibson Business
Centre, Rear of
800 High Road
London N17 ODH
Tel: 0181 365 0222

Heritage Woodcraft
Heritage House
Wheatfield Way
Hinckley Fields
Industrial Estate
Hinckley
Leicestershire
LE10 1YG
Tel: 01455 890 800

**The Natural Wood
Floor**
20 Smugglers Way
London SW18 1EQ
Tel: 0181 871 9771

**Vigers Hardwood
Flooring**
Beechfield Walk
Sewardstone Road
Waltham Abbey
Essex EN9 1AG
Tel: 0181 801 1133

Wallis Wood Floors
Bush House
294 Ongar Road
Writtle
Chelmsford
CM1 3NZ
Tel: 01245 422772

4 Wood Floors
Unit B, Wellington
Industrial Estate
Wellington
Somerset TA21 8ST
Tel: 01823 660912

FURNITURE DESIGNERS AND MAKERS

**David Armstrong
Furniture**
Pitway Lane
Farrington Guerney
Bristol BS18 5TX
Tel: 01761 453117

Clarke & Thomas
1A Fawe Street
London E14
Tel: 0171 987 8145

**Mark Griffiths
Furniture Maker**
Unit 4
Sewells Farm
Barcombe
East Susscx BN8 5TJ
Tel: 01273 401611

**Lion House Antique
Copies**
High Street
Moreton-in-Marsh
Gloucestershire
GL56 OLH
Tel: 01608 652500

**Longpré Cabinet
Makers**
Hatherleigh Farm
Wincanton
Somerset BA9 8AB
Tel: 01963 34356

Mosaic & Stone Tables
The Coach House
Westerham Hill
Westerham
Kent TN16 2EB
Tel: 0181 650 6399

Charles Page
61 Fairfax Road
London NW6 4EE
Tel: 0171 328 9851

Roche-Bobois
421-5 Finchley Road
London NW3 6HJ
Tel: 0171 431 1411

Spareacre Works
Spareacre Lane
Eynsham
Oxfordshire OX8 1NH
Tel: 01865 881214

de Winter Ltd
223 Kensington
Church Street
London W8 7LX
Tel: 0171 229 4949

LIGHTING

Arteluce
31 Lisson Grove
London NW1 6UV
Tel: 0171 258 0600

Bromleighs
Bromleigh House
68 Chapel Road
West Bergholt
Colchester
Essex CO6 3JA
Tel: 01206 241434

**Christopher Wray's
Lighting**
600 King's Road
London SW6 2YW
Tel: 0171 736 8434

**R. Hamilton & Co
Ltd**
Unit G, Quarry
Industrial Estate
Mere
Wiltshire BA12 6LA
Tel: 01747 860088

MOULDINGS AND ORNAMENTATION

Locker & Riley
Capital House
23 Faraday Road
Leigh-on-Sea
Essex SS9 5JU
Tel: 01702 528803

Overmantels
66 Battersea Bridge
Road
London SW11 3AG
Tel: 0171 223 8151

Powell & Brain
18 Finch Close
Shepton Mallet
Somerset BA4 5GA
Tel: 01749 345297

**Stevensons of
Norwich**
Roundtree Way
Norwich NR7 8SQ
Tel: 01603 400824

PAINT AND WALLPAPERS

**Akzo Novel
Decorative Coatings**
PO Box 37
Crown House
Darwen
Lancashire BB3 OBG
Tel: 01254 704951

L. Cornelissen & Son
105 Great Russell Street
London WC1B 3RY
Tel: 0171 636 1045

Dulux
ICI Paints plc
Wexham Road
Slough
Berkshire SL2 5DS
Tel: 01753 550000

Farrow & Ball
249 Fulham Road
London SW3 6HY
Tel: 0171 351 0273

**Harlequin
Wallcoverings Ltd**
Cossington Road
Sileby
Loughborough
Leicestershire
LE12 7RU
Tel: 01509 816575

**International Paint
Ltd**
24-30 Canute Road
Southampton
SO14 3PB
Tel: 01703 226722

John Oliver
33 Pembridge Road
London W11 3HG
Tel: 0171 221 6466

Paint Magic
116 Sheen Road
Richmond
Surrey TW9 1UR
Tel: 0181 940 9799

Papers and Paints Ltd
4 Park Walk
London SW10 OAD
Tel: 0171 352 8626

PICTURE FRAMES

Brian Campbell
5 Peary Place
London E2 0QW
Tel: 0181 983 1109

Framing Workshop
78 Walcot Street
Bath BA1 5BG
Tel: 01225 482748

D. and J. Simons
120-50 Hackney Road
London E2 7QS
Tel: 0171 739 3744

RADIATORS, STOVES AND FIREPLACES

A. Bell & Company Ltd
Kingsthorpe Road
Northampton
NN2 6LT
Tel: 01604 712505

Bisque Ltd
244 Belsize Road
London NW6 4BT
Tel: 0171 328 2225

Caradon Ideal Ltd
PO Box 103
National Avenue
Hull HU5 4JN
Tel: 01482 492251

Classic Stoves Ltd
Blackboys Road
Framfield
East Sussex TN22 5PN
Tel: 01825 890140

The Fireplace Shop
41A Newport
Lincoln LN1 3DN
Tel: 01522 544160

Phil Green & Son
Unit 10
Linton Trading Estate
Bromyard
Herefordshire
HR7 4QT
Tel: 01885 488936

Magnificent Marble
276 High Street
Sutton
Surrey SM1 1PG
Tel: 0181 643 1723

Stanley Cookers Ltd
Abbey Road
Wrexham Industrial
Estate
Wrexham LL13 9RF
Tel: 01978 664555

RESTORATION

Carey B. Restoration
10-12 Hildreth Street
Mews
London SW12 9RZ
Tel: 0181 673 9391

Verdigris
Arch 290
Crown Street
London SE5 0UR
Tel: 0171 703 8373

SANITARYWARE

Bath Craft House
331 Devizes Road
Salisbury
Wiltshire SP2 9JN
Tel: 01722 338999

Czech & Speake
244-54 Cambridge
Heath Road
London E2 9DA
Tel: 0800 919728

C.P. Hart & Sons Ltd
Newnham Terrace
Hercules Road
London SE1 7DR
Tel: 0171 902 1000

Daryl Industries Ltd
Alfred Road
Wallasey
Wirral L44 7HY
Tel: 0151 638 8211

G.E.C. Anderson Ltd
89 Herkomer Road
Bushey
Hertfordshire
WD2 3LS
Tel: 0181 950 1826

Majestic Shower Company
1 North Place
Edinburgh Way
Harlow
Essex CM20 2SL
Tel: 01279 443644

Matki plc
Yate
Bristol BS17 5BR
Tel: 01454 315284

Pegler Ltd
St Catherine's Avenue
Doncaster
South Yorkshire
DN4 8DF
Tel: 01302 560208

STAIRS

Albion Design of Cambridge Ltd
Unit H3, Dales Manor
Business Park
Sawston
Cambridge CB2 4TJ
Tel: 01223 836128

The Cast Iron Shop
394 Caledonian Road
London N1
Tel: 0171 700 3007

Elite Stairs
Unit 7
Blue Lias Marina
Estate
Rugby Road
Stockton
Nr Rugby
Warwickshire
CV23 8HN
Tel: 01926 812060

Hewi (UK) Ltd
Scimitar Close
Gillingham Business
Park
Gillingham
Kent ME8 0RN
Tel: 01634 377688

Malcolm Cole Ltd
10 Nuffield Industrial
Estate
Chantry Park
Cowley Road
Poole
Dorset BH17 7UJ
Tel: 01202 682830

Safety Staircases & Straight Flights
Unit 45, Owen Road
Industrial Estate
Owen Road
Willenhall
West Midlands
WV13 2PX
Tel: 01215 263133

WROUGHT IRON AND METALWORK

Applewood & Perry
Honeybrook Forge
Cranborne Road
Wimborne
Dorset BH21 4HW
Tel: 01202 848676

David Pettitt
13 Langton Street
Chelsea
London SW10 0JL
Tel: 0171 376 3570

The Ironworks
Bay 3
Hornsey Industrial
Properties
Leys Rd
Brockmoor
Brierley Hill
West Midlands
DY5 3UT
Tel: 01384 484200

Jim Lawrence
Traditional Ironwork
Scotland Hall Farm
Stoke by Nayland
Colchester
Essex CO6 4QG
Tel: 01296 263459

Verdigris
Arch 290
Crown Street
London SE5 0UR
Tel: 0171 703 8373

VARIOUS

The Design Council
28 Haymarket Street
London SW14 4SU
Tel: 0171 839 8000

**Crafts Council
Information Unit**
44a Pentonville Road
London N1 9BY
Tel: 0171 806 2500

**National Federation
of Painting and
Decorating
Contractors**
82 New Cavendish
Street
London W1M 9FG
Tel: 0171 580 5404

AUSTRALIA

BATHROOM SUPPLIES

Caroma
Tel: (03) 9354 4355
Fax: (03) 9354 4828
http://www.caroma.co
m.au

CARPETS

Carpet Call
Head office: Lot 2
Village Court
Mulgrave
Tel: (03) 9561 6333
Fax: (03) 9561 8715

Carpet Court
Call 13 13 30 for your
nearest store

CURTAINS

Kresta
Tel: 133 096 (one
number nationwide)

TILES

Academy Tiles
20 Herbet Street
Artamon
NSW 2064
Tel: (02) 9436 3566
Fax: (02) 9436 3577

**Architectural &
Design Centre**
664 Botany Road
Alexandria
NSW 2015
Tel: (02) 9669 6211
Fax: (02) 9693 5952

Romano Tiles
126 Canterbury Road
Kilsyth
VIC 3137
Tel: (03) 9726 4633
Fax: (03) 9720 1568

Index

ACKNOWLEDGMENTS

The author wishes to acknowledge the contribution made by the following at *VT Wonen*: Marita Janssen (editorial director); Iwona de Vos-Tuge (art director); Trudy Bruil (production designer); Rianne Landstra, Frans Bramlage, Marjan Godrie, Petra de Valk, Bastienne van Bockel (stylists); Tessa Jol, Dieuwke Marseille, Esther de Munnik (assistant stylists); Christine van der Hoff (chief sub-editor); Marc Hervermann, Laurens Keff, Karolien Knols (contributing editors); Saskia van der Maat, Jan Willem Papo (assistant editors).